Jeannie helped me, through the pages of this book, to understand that my goal can't be to raise kids who make me proud. Rather, my goal needs to be to help my kids cultivate a relationship with Jesus, who can captivate and shape their hearts.

—Lysa TerKeurst, *New York Times* bestselling author

Rarely do I ever find myself agreeing with everything I read in a book. But this is the book I wish I'd written. Jeannie has given parents a profound gift within its pages.

—Kathie Lee Gifford, cohost, *Today*'s fourth hour

A parenting book that will set you free. Over and over Jeannie reminds me that everything I need and long for I already possess because of what Jesus has done for me.

—Tullian Tchividjian, Pastor, Coral Ridge Presbyterian Church

Filled with grace, wisdom, and practical advice, this book will offer comfort in your parental "failings" and guide you into a Spirit-led, Christ-centered family life.

—Amy Julia Becker, author, *A Good and Perfect Gift*

Moms, grab some girlfriends and read this book together. You'll come away knowing that God isn't just crazy about your kids; he's crazy about you too!

—Jodie Berndt, author, *Praying the Scriptures for Your Children*

Funny and tender, this book is an invitation into the chaos that is motherhood. A useful toolkit, full of grace and wisdom.

—Karen Spears Zacharias, author, *Mother of Rain*

In this lovingly scripted parenting manual, Jeannie bestows a compelling message on parents and children alike as she reminds us that we are unconditionally loved (and liked!) by God in Jesus Christ.

—Kimm Crandall, author, *Christ in the Chaos*

An essential guide for parents who passionately want to lead their children to the heart of God, and who want to raise children who love Jesus with their whole hearts.

—Kathryn Slattery, author, *My Friend Jesus*

Reading Jeannie's writing is like having coffee with a wise friend who truly loves you. Parents of young children will laugh often as they follow her path through biblically supported best-practices for raising great kids.

—Jocelyn (Jill) S. Woolworth, LMFT

A much-needed contribution to the world of parenting resources. Jeannie opens up her life so that parents who are looking for a practical way to guide their children can find comfort, encouragement, and appropriate challenge.

—Meredith Dancause, Adult Life Pastor, Mars Hill Bible Church

Every parent who reads this book will discover deeper personal freedom and grace-based tools with which to love their kids in a whole new way.

—Francie Winslow, MOPS coordinator, speaker, writer

A breath of fresh air for those of us in the parenting trenches. Jeannie provides the tools we all can use in teaching our children about grace and God's love for us all.

—Christy Kyser Truitt, award-winning author of Southern fiction

Jeannie shares how we, in our imperfection, but with God's grace, can raise children who know whose they are and who are filled with the knowledge of God's endless love for them.

—Kris Faasse, Director of Adoption Services, Bethany Christian Services

The best book on practical Christian parenting I have ever read. Cunnion's approach to Christian parenting is practical, accessible, psychologically sound, and developmentally sensitive.

—Hillary R. Bercovici, Senior Fellow, Trinity Institute

Thank you, Jeannie, for opening wide the floodgates to the unconditional love of God and for laying out for us an honest, practical, grace-centered antidote.

—Drew Williams, Senior Pastor, Trinity Church (Greenwich, CT)

This inspired book helps parents protect children from the achieve-aholic treadmill by building a foundation of God's unmerited love and wisdom into their child's life.

—Michael Lee Stallard, author, *Fired Up or Burned Out*

This book offers freedom to burdened moms. Jeannie has beautifully explored profound principles and broken them into doable pieces.

—Courtney DeFeo, owner, Lil Light O' Mine

With a deep understanding of unconditional love, Jeannie makes the word *wholehearted* come alive as an honest, vulnerable, and extraordinary way both to parent and to live.

—Patti Callahan Henry, bestselling novelist

Jeannie Cunnion shows how the good news of the gospel applies to bringing children up and has created a tremendous resource for parents.

—Jessica Thompson, author, *Exploring Grace Together*

parenting the wholehearted child

....

captivating your
child's heart
with God's
extravagant grace

....

jeannie cunnion

ZONDERVAN

Parenting the Wholehearted Child
Copyright © 2014 by Jeannie Cunnion

This title is also available as a Zondervan ebook. Visit www.zondervan.com/ebooks.

Requests for information should be addressed to:

Zondervan, 3900 Sparks Drive SE, *Grand Rapids, Michigan 49546*

Library of Congress Cataloging-in-Publication Data

Cunnion, Jeannie, 1975–
    Parenting the wholehearted child : captivating your child's heart with God's extravagant grace /
Jeannie Cunnion.—First edition.
        pages cm
    Includes bibliographical references.
    ISBN 978-0-310-34084-3 (hardcover)—ISBN 978-0-310-34085-0 (ebook)
    1. Parenting—Religious aspects—Christianity. 2. Child rearing—Religious aspects—Christianity.
3. Christian education of children. 4. Christian education—Home training. I. Title.
    BV4529.C85 2014
    248.8'45—dc23
                                                                          2013037385

Cover design: Brand Navigation
Cover photography: Masterfile
Interior design: David Conn

Printed in the United States of America

14 15 16 17 18 19 20 21 22 /DCI/ 20 19 18 17 16 15 14 13 12 11 10 9 8 7 6 5 4 3 2 1

To my amazing parents,
Bonnie and George Callahan.
Thank you for giving me the indescribable gift
I most desire to give my own children—
the unconditional love of Christ.
I love you so very much.

And to my wonderful husband, Mike.
You are *everything* I pray our boys will become.
I love you, I love being your "wifey,"
and I love stumbling through this parenting thing with you.

•••••••••••••••••••••••••••••••

wholehearted children

Children who live from the freedom found in being wholeheartedly and unconditionally loved (and liked!) by God in Jesus Christ.

Because of God's extravagant grace, wholehearted children are compelled and empowered to love Jesus and love others as he first loved us.

•••••••••••••••••••••••••••••••

contents

foreword

Imagine if God parented us the way we parent our kids:

- "If you answer me back one more time, you will lose your phone for a month."
- "Once you finish your chicken nuggets, then—*maybe*—you can have dessert."
- "You better have a really good reason why you just hit your brother in the face."
- "If I have to ask you one more time to get your shoes on for school, I am going to take you in with just socks."

The more focused we become on perfect parenting, the worse it gets.

The conditions become more defined, the goals more lofty, and the simplest thing—like loving one another the way we are loved—becomes perfectly impossible.

I've been there. Though my intentions were good, my personal and parenting target was way off. Way off, because throughout the day, I focused on what *I* was going to do differently, what *I* could change, what *I* had done wrong, how *I* could please *my* kids, *my* family, *my* friends, *my* career, *my* husband, *my* God more this year than I had last year. It was all up to *me*.

One day, exhausted after a long week and pushing through errands with the kids, I mentioned something to a friend that my daughter was clearly not comfortable with, given her reaction: "Mom! How could you?"

It was the first time I had let her down. I was wrong, and she felt mildly betrayed. Truly, I had tried so hard that day to do my best. To get everything done. To make time for all. To not mess things up. All day long I had tried, but it took only five seconds of bad thinking to meet the enemy: failure. Someone I loved was hurt and disappointed, and the someone I failed was the most precious girl in the whole wide world, and she was looking at me with watery eyes.

"I am so, so sorry, love. So sorry. Please forgive me. I did not know. I never would have mentioned a thing if I knew you felt this way. I never should have said that. Forgive me. I am so sorry."

Her sadness and disappointment grew through her tears.

With a frustrated heart, I let out this cry: "This is all new to me! I have *no* idea what I am doing. Absolutely no idea!"

"What?" Her tears paused. She saw an opening. "Wait—what do you mean?"

I confessed, calmly, "This is all new for me too. I have never had a seven-year-old girl before, and I am going to pray that God gives me what I need to get it right for you."

As shocking as my confession was to her, it was exponentially more frightening to me.

But to my surprise, the awkward crater left by my exasperated admission was eventually filled with the greater comfort of the awesome, naked truth:

I am who God says I am.

I am not a perfect mom.

I never will be.

And that is okay, because he is all I need.

In the way that ocean water slowly fills a hole dug deep in wet sand, *Parenting the Wholehearted Child* fills my days with peace. I cannot thank Jeannie Cunnion enough for being a gift to, and an honest vulnerable voice of, parents. She is able to offer the most refreshing nudges to help us recall all that the Lord says to us and what he has done for us, to set us free from the shackles of unreasonable expectation. Her ability to draw us in, traveling through her day's defeat, challenge, or moment of grace with her kids, is not only relatable but eye-opening. Jeannie's ability to recount an ordinary moment and use it to explore an extraordinary truth leaves me feeling renewed.

This world seeks to take our children away from God, and as a parent desperate to grow my kids to have a heart for God, I have found both solution and peace in Jeannie's writing. It is honest, fresh, not preachy, effortlessly selfless, and wonderfully humble.

In every bit of Jeannie's book is every parent. Join me in reading it over and over again.

—Elisabeth Hasselbeck

acknowledgments

My heart is full, overflowing, with gratitude. There are so many special people I want to honor and thank, so please bear with me. This book would not be possible without each one of them.

To Trinity Church: There aren't words to express my love and thankfulness for you, our church family. I especially want to thank Drew Williams, Hilary Bercovici, and Andy Hayball, who generously gave their time and wisdom to this book in the early days, encouraged me in unimaginable ways, and gave this book wings to fly.

To my dear friend Elisabeth Hasselbeck: Your support and encouragement have daily reminded me of God's extravagant goodness and grace. To say thank you would be wildly insufficient for the gratitude in my heart for your friendship and your passion for the message of this book.

To my amazing agent, Andrew Wolgemuth: You're a godsend, truly. Thank you for believing in this book and partnering with me to share this message. For your wisdom, guidance, and support, I am eternally grateful.

To my incredibly gifted editor, Sandra Vander Zicht: Thank you for guiding me with grace, and shaping this book into something significantly more wonderful than it was when I put it in your wise hands. I'm blessed and honored to be working with you!

To those who played a crucial role in the development of this book, Karen Zacharias Spears, Tullian Tchividjian, Kimm Crandall, Meredith Dancause, Kathryn Slattery, Courtney DeFeo, Jeff and Susan Benner, and Rick and Jill Woolworth: In countless different ways, your encouragement, wisdom, friendship, and support have spurred me on. From the bottom of my heart, thank you.

To Julia and Jeff Eberwein: Thank you for your friendship and for giving my family a haven to live and a peaceful place for me to finish this book after we lost our home in Hurricane Sandy. You've been a vessel of God's outlandish grace in my family's life.

To my wonderful friends who have walked this journey with me and showered me with prayer, wisdom, and encouragement: I wish I could name each one of you, but you know who you are and I am so blessed to call you friend. In particular, I must thank Morella Atkinson, Heidi Hutchinson, and Heather Taylor for being the soul sisters God used to open my heart up to writing this book. God knows how much I love you! And Barb Morris, who made me celebrate what God has done: bless you, sweet friend!

To my in-laws, Gail and Tony Cunnion: No girl could ask for more wonderful grandparents for her children. Because of you, I have an incredible husband and our boys have an extraordinary father. I love you dearly.

To my sisters, Patti Callahan Henry and Barbi Callahan Burris: Patti, you walked this road of writing long before me and have given me priceless wisdom and support. And Barbi, your bottomless well of encouragement has always made me believe anything is possible with God. You have both shaped me in profound ways, and I love you so.

To my three boys, my amazing, beautiful, precious, wild, and life-giving boys who fill my heart up with more love than I ever knew possible: Cal, Brennan, and Owen, I thank God every day for choosing me to be your mom! What an extraordinary gift God has given me in each one of you. Thank you for your patience with me while I wrote this book, and thank you for the countless stories, giggles, and grace you've provided along the way. My ceaseless prayer is that you will always know how wide and how long and how high and how deep is Jesus' wholehearted and unconditional love for you. I love you more and more.

And to Jesus Christ: You've captivated my heart with your love. I thank you for your grace, which has set me free, and for the gift of writing this book to tell of it. I count all things but loss for the surpassing worth of knowing you, Jesus Christ my Lord (Phil. 3:8). All praise and glory to you.

part 1

...

imperfect parents, perfect grace

chapter 1

hanging on by
a thread

We love because he first loved us.
—1 John 4:19

S ome days are easier than others.

At least that's what the flight attendant said, in her most compassionate voice, when she noticed the defeated look on my face. Hungry, tired, and fragile, I'd boarded the late night flight home with my three young children, knowing it wasn't going to be pretty. Within minutes of the cabin door closing, my fellow passengers (I was sure) decided I had no business being a parent as my children relentlessly argued with one another and ignored my every word. It was not one of my finer parenting moments, but it was reflective of one of my typical "I am just hanging on by a thread" kind of days.

Perhaps you know the feeling? It's no wonder. While you are just barely catching your breath under the crushing pressure to get it all right (or else!), the covert message "Do more and try harder to be perfect parents raising perfect kids" awaits you at every corner.

Facebook posts and pristine Christmas cards, though created in love, remind you that everyone else is doing this parenting thing just a little bit better than you. Even in Christian circles, various well-intentioned blogs, books, and speakers have confused the commission to follow Christ's perfect example with the lie that our children's hearts are wholly dependent on our perfect performance as parents. Can I get an amen?

This was a hot topic in my women's Bible study group last fall. So many of our conversations led to our insecurities as mothers and the shame that ensues from feeling like we're never enough or (gasp!) that we're too much. If there was anything we all agreed on, it was how parenting reveals our greatest weaknesses—how emotions and reactions we were once only casually acquainted with (such as anger, impatience, or guilt) suddenly became our closest friends when we became parents.

Indeed, a merciless critic lives in all of us. A critic that causes us to wonder, "How did these precious children get stuck with a parent like me?" A critic that, if we allow it, keeps us in a vicious cycle of "do more, be better, and try harder" to be a perfect mom raising perfect kids. Yes, I know that merciless critic all too well.

My Quest for Perfection

My quest for perfection is ironic, really, because I was raised in a very "grace-full" home. I was the youngest of three girls. "Preacher's kids," we were called, because our father was the pastor of a large Presbyterian church. My sisters are eighteen months apart, then I came along ten years later, and by the time I joined the family, grace had taken its rightful place in our home. (I'm told it wasn't always that way.) I knew, growing up, that I was unconditionally loved, because my parents embraced me in my failure just as quickly as they embraced me in my success.

But being a preacher's kid, I'm sure, had a significant influence on my desire to be perfect, since it often felt like all eyes were on me, and my parents' reputation seemed to be at stake with each poor decision I made. This pressure, however, didn't come from within our home. I inherited it from elsewhere.

Yes, grace is so countercultural and so counterintuitive that if we don't water our kids' souls with it every day, they can so easily get tangled up in the world's web of perfection and performing for us and for God.

Somewhere along the line, I began to link accomplishment to acceptance. I guess you could say I'm wired for earning and deserving, but aren't we all? As long as I can remember, I've been achievement driven. I desperately wanted to get it right, whatever "it" was. And, of course, that's impossible. I got it wrong, a lot. Terribly and horribly wrong. So while shame was brewing on the inside, performance was reigning on the outside, and my worth was becoming more and more dependent on who people *thought* I was instead of on who God says I am in Christ.

Then when I became a mother, my quest for perfection only intensified.

From the moment I found out I was pregnant, I was determined to do this parenting thing well. Very, very well. At the time, we lived in an apartment in New York City, so one of the first things my husband, Mike, and I did was walk across the street to

> My worth was becoming more and more dependent on who people *thought* I was instead of on who God says I am in Christ.

the bookstore to scoop up a *huge* pile of books. Some of the books I bought were about eating healthfully (none of which I followed particularly well, which is why I looked like Shrek during my pregnancy), a few were about what to expect while pregnant so that I could follow my unborn child's development closely, and only one book was about childbirth (because I didn't want to know much more than how to clearly ask for an epidural at the very moment I felt a twinge of pain).

And then I read, and I read, and I read.

Nine months later, Cal entered this world. Someone once said that having a baby is like watching your heart walk around outside of your body. Indeed it is, and I assume it always will be. Tiny Cal immediately stole my heart right out of my chest, and he still walks around with it in his little hands today.

With every new stage of Cal's life, I read a few more books. I read everything from how to survive the first six sleep-deprived months to how to tackle the "terrible twos" (which should actually be called "the twos have nothing on the threes"). But reading wasn't the only thing I was doing. We also found time to add two more little guys to our brood. Brennan came three years after Cal, and Owen came two years after Brennan. So in the blink of an eye, we had three boys under six, and although I was trying hard—so very hard—to parent perfectly, it didn't take long for things to unravel. Imagine a tsunami roaring through your home. That's what it felt like on most days in the Cunnion household.

Most of the parenting tricks I'd read about were no longer working, and the ones that did work brought only short-term change. The sibling arguments, the inconsolable infant's crying, and the glorious temper tantrums could not be controlled by the parenting tips and tactics I was implementing with precision. So I started using my "big voice" a lot (which really just means I was yelling, but it made me feel so much better to call it my big voice). The truth was, I was yelling at my children to stop yelling. I was a girl undone, so much so that my temper tantrums rivaled theirs. Imagine how effective that was.

Around this same time, Cal was given a chance to describe our family in a class project. I didn't know this class exercise was on the horizon or I would have been on my best behavior in the days preceding it. But God had another plan, one that would convict and change my heart.

I assume the teacher intended this little book to be a special keepsake, but that wasn't the case for our family. The front cover of the book reads "My Family" and has an adorable picture of Cal in his classroom. Inside the book is a typed note from Cal's teacher, who evidently wrote (verbatim) the words that Cal spoke when he was asked to describe us. The typed note reads, "Brennan cries a lot! 'Cause he sometimes gets sick and sometimes he gets well when he cries. Mommy just raises her voice when I'm not a good listener. She checks on the computer too. Daddy works on the computer too. He checks out *Thomas the Tank Engine* for me. Now that's the end of my story."

His words hit me like an arrow to the heart. I remember holding that card and sobbing, "How could that be *my* child's story when I've been trying so hard to get it right?" Though I was devastated to see myself and our family through Cal's eyes, his card was the only thing strong enough to pry my eyes open to the painful truth I'd been trying so hard to avoid: perfectionism had become an idol in my life, and it was stealing all of our joy.

While I had surrendered my heart to Jesus in my childhood, I hadn't been living in the freedom of his grace, and I definitely wasn't parenting our kids in the freedom of his grace. I may have started my day with a prayer that went something like, "Lord, I am yours. I lay this day at your feet and ask you to make my heart your home," but I quickly got lost in a stream of self-reliance. Rather than casting my anxiety on Jesus (1 Peter 5:7) and trusting in him to direct my path (Prov. 3:5–6), I was relying only on my own effort and only on my own understanding. In all of my reading of those countless parenting books, my goal was to fix, to control, and to perfect our family.

And why? Because long ago I bought stock in the expression, "Your life is God's gift to you, and what you do with your life is your gift to God." I thought my gift to God was trying to be, act, think, and parent perfectly. Somewhere along the line, I stopped believing that, as C. S. Lewis put it, "God doesn't want something from us. He simply wants us." So naturally I became determined to perfect my behavior, rather than allow God's grace to transform my heart. I was determined to perfect our children's behavior too, rather than captivate their hearts with his love and grace. Better said, I was focused on teaching my kids what they had to do for Jesus rather than teaching them what Jesus has already done for them through his death on the cross and his resurrection. I wasn't giving my kids the grace that God so lavishly gives us in Jesus Christ.

All the while, Jesus was patiently waiting for me to listen just long enough to hear his gracious voice whispering, "Jeannie, my beloved child, *I* am your perfection. You can stop performing, and you can stop pretending; that is what my grace is for."

And once I was finally able to surrender, which didn't happen easily and didn't happen overnight, my heart found the rest it craved in the glorious truth of 2 Corinthians 12:9: "My grace is sufficient for you, for my power is made perfect in weakness." His grace, his saving grace, is sufficient, and his divine power is displayed and even made perfect in my weaknesses as a mom.

The burden, the angst, the striving—exchanged for joy, for hope, for peace. All extraordinary gifts given when our hearts surrender to his grace.

Fully Known and Fully Loved

As his grace began to transform my heart, it also began to transform my parenting. Gradually my quest to raise perfect children was transformed into a desire to raise "wholehearted children"—children who live from the freedom found in being wholeheartedly and unconditionally loved (and liked!) by God in Jesus Christ.

What I now wanted was to raise children who understand that they are fully known and fully loved, and who experience the fullness of life and the power of God that we read of in Ephesians 3:17–19 (NLV): "I pray that Christ may live in your hearts by faith. I pray that you will be filled with love. I pray that you will be able to understand how wide and how long and how high and how deep His love is. I pray that you will know the love of Christ. His love goes beyond anything we can understand. I pray that you will be filled with God Himself."

We all, parents and children alike, have an innate longing to feel fully known and fully loved. This longing, designed by God, was planted deep within us for a purpose—to make us thirst for his glory and his presence in every piece of our being. He is the only one who can truly satisfy our souls. In the piercing words of St. Augustine, "You have made us for yourself, O Lord, and our hearts are restless until they rest in you." God created us for himself, and we will search endlessly and hopelessly until we realize that our hearts were made to enjoy the fullness of his love for us.

Teaching this truth to my children became my new purpose, because only when we experience his extravagant grace and wholehearted love for us are we then enlivened to obey the greatest commandment in the Law: "'Love the Lord your God with all your heart and with all your soul and with all your mind.' This is the first and greatest commandment. And the second is like it: 'Love your neighbor as yourself'" (Matt. 22:37–39).

Raising children who love Jesus and love one another does not result from our doing more and trying harder to be perfect parents raising perfect kids. There is only one perfect parent—our heavenly Father. And there is only one perfect child—Jesus Christ, his Son. So while perfectionist parenting teaches children that they are capable of loving God and one another as the Law demands, parenting with grace teaches children that God's love for them is based not on their perfect keeping of the law but rather on Jesus' perfect keeping of it for them. Only Jesus can and does love perfectly. Wholeheartedly.

Wholehearted children, therefore, are children who grow up with a keen awareness of just how wholly dependent they are on Jesus' wholehearted love for them. This is the best news of all because it fixes our gaze on a God whose wholeheartedness covers over (and meets us in) our half-heartedness.

> Only Jesus can and does love perfectly. Wholeheartedly.

Knowing that they are fully known and fully loved allows our children to live in the freedom and fullness of Jesus' unconditional love for them without the burden of perfection, performance, and pretending. This, my friend, is extravagant grace, and in experiencing this grace, our hearts are captivated and transformed. The grace of God is the power that compels us (2 Cor. 5:14). "We love because he first loved us" (1 John 4:19). God's love given to us in Jesus Christ precedes and produces our love for others.

And this is why our starting place in parenting wholehearted children is the extravagant grace of God. If we long to see our kids grow in a vibrant friendship with Jesus, and grow in his likeness to be his love and his light in this broken world, let us put the ledgers away and give our kids grace upon grace (John 1:16).

chapter 2

grace, our starting place

Dear friends, let us love one another, for love comes from God. Everyone who loves has been born of God and knows God.... This is how God showed his love among us: He sent his one and only Son into the world that we might live through him.... And so we know and rely on the love God has for us. God is love.

—1 John 4:7, 9, 16

It was a beautiful fall day, and our family was headed out the door to the elementary school pumpkin patch festival. Mike had some things he had to drop off at the festival, so he drove to the school while the kids and I made the ten minute bike ride.

As Cal, Owen, and I approached a busy street corner, I noticed Brennan was lagging too far behind. I asked Cal to stay put while I crept backward to assist Brennan. After a few seconds of helping Brennan get back on track, I looked ahead, only to find Cal nowhere in sight. My heart started racing, but I assured myself Cal had chosen to go ahead to the festival because he was anxious to see his friends.

When Brennan, Owen, and I arrived at the school bike rack, I didn't see Cal's bike, nor did I see him anywhere on the playground where his friends were playing. Starting to panic, I scanned the crowd of people to no avail. Moments later I found a kind friend who offered to keep Brennan and Owen while I continued to search for Cal in earnest. After several minutes of searching, with fear consuming my every thought, I called Mike and then I made the call no parent should ever have to make: I called the police.

As the harsh reality set in that Cal was definitely not at the school, a good friend advised me to backtrack our path in case Cal had gotten scared and decided to find his way home. Although I thought there was no way Cal would have attempted to go home without us, I got back on my bike and headed home in a complete haze, crying out loud and pleading, "Lord, please protect my son."

The five-minute bike ride felt like an endless journey, but as I entered our neighborhood, I saw Cal in the distance. He was walking up a hill, no shoes or socks on his feet, crying and scared. I began yelling, "Cal, Cal, Mommy is here. Come this way, Cal!" and I raced faster on my bike to get to him, desperate to hold him in my arms and cover him in my love.

As I held my sobbing son, he began apologizing for disobeying and going ahead of me on his bike. "Mommy," he cried, "I was so scared, and I'm sorry for not listening to you. I was so excited to get to the festival, but when I got there, I felt bad about going ahead, so I turned around to come back to you. But I got lost, Mommy. I'm so sorry."

With a breaking but relieved heart, I replied, "Cal, I love you so much. I'm not mad at you. I'm just happy Jesus led you safely home. I was praying he would keep you safe while I searched everywhere for you. No need for apologies right now, baby. I'm just so happy to have you back in my arms. That is all that matters."

I didn't want to let go. I wanted to keep his heart pressed against mine, my tears mingling with his. Whatever he'd just done wrong paled in comparison with the joy in my heart to have him back in my arms. My love for him was unfazed by his wrong actions. By his disobedience. By his going ahead of me, trying to do life without me. He was home—that was all that mattered.

Later that night after the kids were in bed, I reflected on the events of the day and was reminded of the parable of the prodigal son in the gospel of Luke, chapter 15, about the rebellious son who runs away from home and squanders his inheritance, and the father who graciously welcomes his son home upon his return. Luke describes the son's return this way: "But while he was still a long way off, his father saw him and was filled with compassion for him; he ran to his son, threw his arms around him and kissed him" (Luke 15:20).

The unconditional love and absolute acceptance the father had for his son in this parable symbolizes the unconditional love and absolute acceptance our heavenly Father pours out on us through his Son, Jesus Christ. This parable is a portrait of God's grace, a poignant reminder that when we are in Christ, there is no condemnation, no shame, no, "That's what you get for disobeying me." There is only, "I am so happy to have you back in my arms. I love you so much!" His arms are open. He is running to meet you, to pull you up, to hold you close. To captivate you with his grace.

Grace Defined

Because grace is the central message of the Bible and the foundation of parenting a wholehearted child, I want to explore some of the ways in which Scripture guides us in defining, understanding, and responding to grace.

According to Scripture, grace is God's unmerited favor and undeserved love toward us because of the atoning sacrifice and finished work of his Son, Jesus Christ. Said more simply, grace is Jesus Christ himself.

Another way grace can be defined—and this is my favorite way to think about it—is "one-way love." Paul Zahl, in *Grace in Practice*, writes, "God's one-way love is a love that acts independent of all response to it yet at the same time elicits a response."[1] This one-way love persists when we resist and pursues us in our most unlovable moments. Grace is a love that knows the depth of your heart, all the muck and mire, and loves you the same. Yes, grace is a love that know no limits—it is God's unending and unrestrained affection for and acceptance of you. It is the one-way love God showed us in Christ, *while we were still sinners*, and by which we are saved (Rom. 5:8).

Grace in Parenting

What significance does grace hold for us as parents? How does it inform and influence our role as mom or dad? The implications are huge. Grace takes a red sharpie marker and writes "Done!" over our "do more, try harder, and be better" list for pleasing God and earning his favor and acceptance. Grace says, "Cease striving and know that *I* am God" (Ps. 46:10 NASB). We can cease striving for what is already ours in Christ Jesus: God's pleasure, God's favor, and God's unconditional acceptance of us. His acceptance is given not because of how well we did (or didn't) parent our children today but because of what Jesus Christ has already accomplished for us on the cross through his death and resurrection. God's eternal love, favor, pleasure, and acceptance are

> Grace says, "Cease striving and know that *I* am God."

yours, right now. Not once you become a better parent raising better kids. Right now, just as you are, covered in the righteousness of Christ. Don't stop listening after the diagnosis of God's law: you're a sinner in need of a savior. Pay attention to the cure: Christ has made you a perfectly righteous and beloved child of God. You are an imperfect parent covered by the perfection of Christ.

"Grace, our starting place" therefore means that we make this radical, one-way love of God the foundation of our parenting. In doing so, our kids are also set free to hear the diagnosis of God's law (you're a sinner in need of a savior) *and* to see themselves for who they are in Christ: perfectly righteous and beloved children of God. They are fully known and fully loved by a God who not only created them in his image but also gives them his Spirit to empower them to live in his likeness—Christlikeness. This does not indicate that we become divine in any sense; rather it only indicates that we are indwelt by God through the gift of his Spirit and may, therefore, share in his likeness by obeying his commandments. We will dive deeper into the waters of Christlikeness in chapter 10. Here I simply want to highlight the different roles that law and grace play in our parenting. And in our entire lives, for that matter.

So don't miss this—just because we teach our kids how to live in obedience to his commandments does not mean they are then equipped or enabled to obey those laws. In fact, one of the main characteristics of God's law is this: knowledge of God's law does not beget the ability to obey God's law. While God's law is indeed holy, righteous, and good (Rom. 7:12), and is perfect, trustworthy, and more precious than gold (Ps. 19:7–10), the law alone cannot inspire obedience and change the human heart.

What does transform, inspire, and enable the human heart is God's radical grace. The Spirit of God carries the grace of God into the hearts of the children of God to convict us of our sin, transform our hearts, and inspire us to grateful obedience.

The laws, or the rules, that we teach our kids will only show our kids what obedience—or Christlikeness—looks like, but the grace of God transforms the heart and inspires them to grow and share in his likeness.

As Elyse Fitzpatrick so beautifully explains in *Counsel from the Cross*, "When we lose the centrality of the cross, Christianity morphs into a religion of self-improvement and becomes about us, about our accomplishments, and about getting our act together. We become people who ask WWJD (What would Jesus do?) without ever considering the gospel or WDJD (What did Jesus do?)."[2]

> Parenting from the cross requires that we first give our kids the good news of WDJD before we ask them to live in light of WWJD.

Parenting from the cross requires that we first give our kids the good news of WDJD (What did Jesus do?) before we ask them to live in light of WWJD (What would Jesus do?). What Jesus already did—"Immense in mercy and with an incredible love, he embraced us. He took our sin-dead lives and made us alive in Christ" (Eph. 2:4–5 MSG)—inspires us to act in grateful obedience to the commandments of Christ. It's true. A heart that soaks in his grace is a heart that delights in his law.

In experiencing the wholehearted love of God, we are moved beyond ourselves. To be wholeheartedly loved in our most unlovable moments doesn't just compel us. It wrecks us. It drives us. Right to Jesus. To trust in his word and obey his commands. That's what his grace can do to us and to our children.

To be clear, "Grace, our starting place" is not a new parenting technique. My friend Kimm Crandall, author of *Christ in the Chaos: How the Gospel Changes Motherhood*, once shared these wise words: "If we give our children grace today with the intent of changing their behavior, are we really giving them grace? No, we are merely making grace into a new parenting rule, another law that tells us, 'Do this and you will get that.' Grace has no expectations. Grace gives without getting."

We give our kids grace to teach them what God did to win their hearts, their love. That is our crucial role as parents. A role, might I add, that research reveals is not to be taken lightly.

Faith That Sticks

I recently read an excellent book titled *Sticky Faith* by Kara Powell and Chap Clark that examines how parents can grow within their children a deep faith that sticks. Their extensive research, which astounded me, concludes that "40 to 50 percent of kids who graduate from a church or youth group will fail to stick with their faith in college."[3]

Based on this research, and an abundance of other studies that echo it, we know that we must be intentional in helping our children come to know and experience Jesus. We must demonstrate a faith that our children desire to experience, not flee. Discipling our kids in the truth and grace of Jesus Christ must be an intentional pursuit.

This knowledge then raises important questions like, How can I be intentional in discipling my kids? and, What does discipling even mean?

What Is a Disciple?

Since the word *disciple* conjures up some serious stereotypes, let's start by defining it. A disciple is, quite simply, a learner. A disciple can also be described as a follower or an apprentice. So the reality is that every child is a disciple, especially of their parents. Whether we realize it or not, whether we like it or not, we are all discipling our children. The big question is, In what are they being discipled? Are we discipling our kids in the grace and unconditional love of Jesus Christ, or are we discipling them in the school of law and good works?

Scripture tells us that God invites us into a faith relationship through the grace of Jesus Christ. So we as parents have to be purposeful in building on grace if we desire our kids to know and love the real Jesus.

Proceed with Hope

Before it begins to sound as though the responsibility of raising kids who love Jesus falls entirely on our shoulders as parents, I want to add a strong dose of hope to the equation.

Please hear this important truth: our children will not come to love Jesus *because* of us. In fact, I can say with great confidence that on many days my kids will fall in love with Jesus in spite of me. Though I am God's beloved, infinitely adored, and unconditionally loved child who is continually being transformed into his image by the power of his Holy Spirit, I am a sinner in need of my Savior. Rest assured, there are still plenty of moments when I find myself walking that fine line between holy living and (attempted) perfect living and I wonder, "Why on earth did Jesus entrust these children to me?" If I didn't have those feelings, I'd be living in denial. There are also plenty of days when the merciless critic inside my head tells me to give up on raising wholehearted children because of certain behaviors they are displaying. (They are indeed human, after all, and ever in need of grace.)

> Our children will not come to love Jesus *because* of us.

So, yes, while it's important that you and I be purposeful in discipling our kids and building a foundation of grace on which they can come to know and love Jesus, we are not *responsible* for transforming their hearts. We can give grace, and we can show grace. But our giving and showing are not what penetrate and transform our children's hearts.

Mom and Dad, take a long, deep breath of relief as you let these words of truth marinate in your soul: God, and God alone, transforms the human heart. His Spirit, the Holy Spirit, carries the grace you give and the grace you show like a renowned surgeon to the heart of your child. Yes, you can be a vessel of his grace and a reflection of his love, but you do not have to play God's role. So breathe. Maybe even smile. God's got this.

As Paul notes, "And I am certain that God, who began the good work within you, will continue his work until it is finally finished on the day when Christ Jesus returns.... May you always be filled with the fruit of your salvation — the righteous character produced in your life by Jesus Christ — for this will bring much glory and praise to God" (Phil. 1:6, 11 NLT). In Christ alone is a child's heart transformed, the love affair begun, and Christlike character produced.

Our role as parents is to keep praying our children back into the palms of Jesus' nail-pierced hands. We can pray for wisdom from God as we seek to be the vessel by which our children experience his unrelenting love and mercy (James 1:5). We can pray for obedience to the commission to disciple our children in the truth of Christ, and to teach them what really matters. We can pray that our children grow a heart that is tender to his voice and passionate about his Word. And we can proceed with hope, resting in his grace for us and trusting in the Holy Spirit to captivate their hearts with his love.

Let us not forget that as much as we love our kids, Jesus loves them more. And as much as we want for our kids, Jesus wants for them more. This is the good news we can rest in. Our kids have been entrusted into our care for a short while so that we can point them back to the Creator, Lover, and Redeemer of their souls.

One of the most wonderful ways we can point our kids to Jesus is by accepting our identity as beloved children of God and then affirming our children's identity as his beloved children too. So I want to spend the next chapter looking at the awesome privilege we have of teaching our children about their identity in Christ, recognizing that this will have a profound impact on their desire to put their trust in him and grow in his likeness.

chapter 3

he calls me beloved

I'll call nobodies and make them somebodies;
I'll call the unloved and make them beloved.
In the place where they yelled out, "You're
nobody!" they're calling you "God's
living children."

—Romans 9:25 MSG

For Mike's birthday present last year, I told Brennan to pour out his love on Daddy. I explained, "Brennan, Daddy said that the only thing he wants for his birthday is your love. So go give him a big hug and all of the love in your heart. That will make him the happiest daddy in the whole wide world."

Brennan furrowed his brow. "But Mommy, if I give Daddy all the love in my heart, I won't have any left to give you." (I love this about my sweet Brennan; he always thinks so deeply about things.)

I pulled Brennan close, realizing that this was a wonderful moment to teach him about the bottomless well of Jesus' love for us. I explained, "Brennan, every time we pour out love for one another, Jesus fills us right back up with more love. You can rest assured that if you give Daddy all of your love, Jesus will fill your heart right back up with more love to share with Mommy."

Brennan smiled and asked, "So it's impossible for Jesus to run out of love?"

"Yes, baby," I assured, "because Jesus doesn't just have love, he *is* love. Overflowing, unstoppable, and unconditional love."

Our Identity: Created and Redeemed by Love

Just as our love for our children began even before they were born, so did God's amazing love for us. Just as we plotted and prepared and anticipated the birth of our first child, so did our loving heavenly Father. Carefully and creatively he crafted a world for us to live in, a place of beauty that would nourish us and enable us to flourish. And when everything was ready, he created humanity, in his own image, so that we would know we belonged to him, and we would love him (Gen. 1–2).

However, in Genesis 3 we witness the destruction of this perfect relationship, when Adam and Eve, the first humans, tragically chose to disobey and rebel against God. In that moment, all of humanity became tainted with sin and things were no longer as they were meant to be. We became enslaved to our sinful nature — spiritually dead (Rom. 5:12–21).

> Our identity comes from Christ, who both created us in love and redeemed us in love, making us beloved children of God.

But God, in his great mercy and compassion, took the initiative to reconcile us to himself. To forgive our sin and heal our brokenness. To bring us back into a loving relationship with him. And the only way home, as prophesied throughout the Old Testament, was through the perfect sacrifice of his Son, Jesus Christ. As we read in 2 Corinthians 5:21, "God made him who had no sin to be sin for us, so that in him we might become the righteousness of God." Our identity, then, comes from Christ, who both created us in love and redeemed us in love, making us beloved children of God (John 1:12).

Who Jesus *Really* Is

In John 14:6, Jesus says, "I am the way and the truth and the life. No one comes to the Father except through me." Who Jesus really is then is both extravagant love and the only way to abundant and eternal life. He is the only one who can fill the God-shaped hole in our hearts. And he is our great rescuer.

Think about the word *rescuer* for a moment. What image does that conjure up? For me, I picture someone who comes in and saves the day. Someone who parts the sea. Someone who calms a raging storm. Someone who raises the dead. Someone who gave his life for mine long before I had anything to give to him in return.

Teaching our children about our own need for a rescuer and the free gift of salvation by grace through faith is how we teach them that their salvation and acceptance before our perfect, holy, and righteous God is not based on how well they obey, or how often they do what Jesus would do. They are accepted and made right with God because of Christ and his righteousness alone. They have God's unconditional and extravagant love not because they were respectful of Mommy or kind to their sibling but because of Jesus' finished work on the cross to redeem and restore them.

Another important, but often overlooked, piece in helping our children understand who Jesus is, is teaching them about the remarkable personality of Christ, the God-man. Oh, how I love his personality, "playful, cunning, fierce, impatient with all that is religious, kind, creative, irreverent, and funny."[4] Growing up, I often heard my parents speak of the personality of Jesus, and it had an extraordinary impact on me. They led me to think of Jesus as not

> We are accepted and made right with God because of Christ and his righteousness alone.

just my God but also my friend. A friend who was interested not in my "religiousness" but in having a relationship with me. See, if we read the Bible with an eye for Jesus' extraordinary personality, we will find that while he was perfect and holy, he was anything but the dull and removed God-man we find in so much of the artwork that depicts him. Especially when introducing our children to Jesus, the God-man, we want to personalize Christ as someone to whom our kids can relate, someone who walked this earth, experienced all that they experience, and knows the depths of their struggles, their desires, their joy, and their pain. Yes, he is Mighty God, Everlasting Father, and Prince of Peace, but let us not forget that he is also the very best friend we will ever have.

Who Does Jesus Say I Am?

A few years ago I signed up for Beth Moore's *Believing God* Bible study, having no idea that God was about to get very busy with me and my inability to see myself covered in the perfection of Christ. In one particular lesson, Beth taught on "believing you are who God says you are,"[5] and God used her words, in that moment, to open my eyes to who I am in Christ.

Think about this for a moment. Who does God say you are? Beth explained that *in Christ*, God says you are loved, blessed, chosen, adopted, accepted, redeemed, and forgiven (Eph. 1:3–8).

While I was sitting among fifteen other women soaking up this amazing message for myself, I was reminded how awesome it is that I can also bathe my children in these life-giving, joy-inducing, shame-lifting, and heart-strengthening truths. The author of Hebrews reminds us, "It is good for our hearts to be strengthened by grace!" (Heb. 13:9), so no mat-

> We can encourage our kids by teaching them who are they in Christ.

ter where we are or what we're doing, God is inviting us to strengthen our kids' hearts with the grace of God—to speak his words of life and love over them. When we are walking along the sidewalk, playing in the yard, snuggling at bedtime, riding in the car, or speaking into their sadness, we can encourage our kids by teaching them who they are in Christ.

The Bible is salted with God's expression of delight in his children. Here are just a few examples:

- He loves you just as you are—his love is unconditional (Rom. 5:8; Eph. 3:18–20).
- You are fully known and fully loved. He knows everything about you, and he accepts you, understands you, and likes you (Ps. 139; Luke 12:7).
- You are the apple of his eye (Ps. 17:8).
- You are a King's kid (1 John 3:1).
- He is *for* you (Rom. 8:31–32; Jer. 29:11–13; 1 Cor. 2:9).
- You are his masterpiece (Eph. 2:8–11).
- You bring him great joy (Mark 1:11).
- He delights in you; he celebrates over you (Zeph. 3:17).
- You are a friend of God (John 15:12–15).
- He calls you beloved (Rom. 9:25).
- You are loved, blessed, chosen, adopted, accepted, redeemed, and forgiven (Eph. 1:3–8).

How awesome is it that we can encourage ourselves and our kids with these truths? When the internal and external voices proclaim, "You're not enough. You're not measuring up. You should be more like this, or you should be more like that. You are a disappointment," we can remember this: the only one who gets to define us is God, and he calls us beloved sons and daughters.

As the late Brennan Manning observes, "His love is gratuitous in a way that defies our imagination. It is for this reason that we can proclaim with theological certainty in the power of the Word: God loves you as you are and not as you should be! Do you believe this? That God loves you beyond worthiness and unworthiness, beyond fidelity and infidelity, that he loves you in the morning sun and the evening rain, that he loves you without caution, regret, boundary, limit or breaking point?"[6]

> "God loves you as you are and not as you should be! Do you believe this?"

Because of Jesus, God loves me just as I am, not as I should be. God loves you just as you are, not as you should be. I want this truth to take root deep down in our souls, because our high calling as parents is to instill in our children this wondrous knowledge that Jesus knows everything about them and unconditionally loves them, accepts them, understands them, enjoys them, and likes them exactly as they are! They are fully known and fully loved. Just imagine the repercussions of raising a generation of children who live from the freedom found in being wholeheartedly loved (and liked!) by God, in Jesus Christ, in this intimate, personal way.

Accepting Christ's Acceptance

At this point you may be wondering, "Okay, I see why grace needs to be my starting place, but how do I begin to apply this knowledge to raising a wholehearted child?" This was my burning question when I first began to loosen my grip on perfection and allow grace to infuse my parenting.

So here it is, the answer to the burning question and the truth I have to surrender to on a daily basis: we parent a wholehearted child by first accepting God's wholehearted acceptance of us in Jesus Christ.

It's a lot like what the flight attendant tells you to do in the event of an emergency on an airplane. "Before trying to put the oxygen mask on your child, you need to put your oxygen mask on first." God's grace is the oxygen mask we are talking about here. Before you can give grace and show grace to your children, you first need to accept and enjoy the grace God has freely given *you* in Christ Jesus.

It sounds simple, right? The problem is that surrendering to grace can feel impossible. And let me assure you, I took the long and winding road to accepting my acceptance.

I was saved by grace at the age of eight when the Holy Spirit stirred my heart to repentance. My mom took me to the movie theater in Deerfield Beach, Florida, to see the Billy Graham movie *The Prodigal.* When we got home, I crawled into bed, overwhelmed by the desire to give my life to Christ. When my mom came in to tuck me in, I asked her to pray with me. I wanted to put my trust in Jesus and accept him as my Savior.

In that moment, I was saved by grace through faith. Since that moment, I have lived in con-

> On most days I acted like Jesus' final three words on the cross were "Make me proud."

fidence that I am his and he is mine. I know that full well. He paid my ransom. He fulfilled the law that I could never fulfill. By grace I am saved from condemnation, saved from punishment for my sins, saved from eternal separation from God.

What I struggled to understand was this: by grace I am *accepted*. It was so much easier for me to think of being saved by grace than it was to think of being accepted by grace after I gave my life to God. I fought the unconditionality of his love.

On most days I acted like Jesus' final three words on the cross were "Make me proud" instead of the actual three words he exhaled, "It is finished." This is how the conversation between us would go:

Me: Jesus, I am such a mess. I can't believe you chose to die for a sinner like me. Thank you for giving your life for mine. Thank you for your divine exchange of my sins for your righteousness. It makes no sense that you, my King, would die for me ... but you did. And I love you. Now I will make you proud of me. I will make your death on the cross worth it.

Jesus: Jeannie, my sweet child. I chose the nails for you because I love you. I am already proud of you. There is nothing you can do to make me love you any less, and there is nothing you can do to make me love you any more. I want you to rest in that.

Me: I know, I know. And I'm thankful. But you *died* for me. A painful, gruesome, humiliating death. And what do I do? I still sin. I still take my husband for granted; I still lose my patience with my kids; I still think awful thoughts about the person who rushed to get in front of me in the grocery store line. Oh, and I'm not very good at loving my enemies. I'm good at faking it, but deep down, I'm not always feelin' the love.

Jesus: I know. And I love you. I accept you just as you are. In me, you are worthy just as you are. In me, you are enough just as you are. I have you covered. And I am still at work, transforming you into my image.

Me: I know, Jesus. But just listen—I still want to make you proud. I want to do something, anything, to show you how thankful I am for what you did for me. I will keep trying to do more, be better, and work harder to make you proud.

Jesus: Jeannie, my beloved Jeannie. All I want is you. Walk with me. Keep company with me. Pray to me. Enjoy my presence. Delight in

my kindness. Dance in my faithfulness. Everything that matters—
everything that reflects holy, Christlike living—will flow from your
loving me and abiding in me. Cease striving and know that I am
God [Ps. 46:10]. Surrender to my grace, to my unconditional, unrelenting, never-ceasing love for you, just as you are.

So you can see, while I have never doubted my salvation, I
have questioned my worthiness and acceptance before God. In fact,
I have spent most of my life trying to be acceptable before God
through my good works. Through my parenting, through my calling in adoption work, through service in my church, through my
role as a daughter, sister, friend, and wife, I tried to prove to God
that I was enough, that I was committed to him, that I was grateful
for his sacrifice for me, that I was worthy! I did everything short of
serenade God with my own rendition of "You're Gonna Love Me."

Simply said, I refused to rest in the promise we read in Ephesians
2:8–10, "For it is by grace you have been saved, through faith—and
this is not from yourselves, it is the gift of God—not by works, so
that no one can boast. For we are God's handiwork, created in Christ
Jesus to do good works, which God prepared in advance for us to do."

I think of the countless nights, during my time of perfectionist
parenting, that I put the kids to bed, then curled up on the couch
and wept. I was drowning in self-pity and despair from the guilt and
shame of not being a "perfect" mom. I would rehash all of the things
I did wrong that day, the ways in which I wasn't 1,000 percent available to them, the times I yelled or lost my temper when they misbehaved, the times I got frustrated or mad because my three-year-old
was—gasp!—acting like a three-year-old.

Mike would come home from work to find me on the couch,
deeply engrossed in my little pity party, and would assure me I was
the greatest mom in the whole entire world and our kids were blessed
to have me. But that wasn't enough. His words were kind and loving

and wonderful, but they weren't enough. The guilt and the shame of being an imperfect person of faith still weighed heavily on me.

Looking back on those days, I now realize God was protecting my heart from resting in words of affirmation from my husband, my mom, or my best friend, who would all assure me I was awesome. God, in his great compassion and mercy, did not allow me to find my peace from others. He wanted my eyes fixed on him—the only one who truly satisfies my soul, the only real hope I have. He wanted me to rest in his selflessness, in his patience, in his goodness, in his wild love for me. And he knew that only when I realized that by grace alone I am not only saved but also accepted would I find peace and rest and real joy.

> It's not about what we do. It's about what his grace does through us when we surrender to his wholehearted acceptance of us.

I know that now. And when that truth pierced my heart, it set me free.

Of course I still have moments of doubt and defeat, but now I freely confess those feelings. I recognize the voice of condemnation (which is not the voice of Jesus), and I don't cling to the guilt and shame. Instead, I confess it out loud and remember his final three words on the cross: "It is finished." And I am set free.

I am a wholehearted child of God. And that changes everything. As Brennan Manning writes in *The Furious Longing of God*, "The wild unrestricted love of God is not simply an inspiring idea. When it imposes itself on mind and heart with the stark reality of ontological truth, it determines why and at what time you get up in the morning, how you pass your evenings, how you spend your weekends, what you read, and who you hang with; it affects what breaks your heart, what amazes you, and what makes your heart happy."[7]

Until we accept God's wild, unrestricted love and absolute

acceptance of us, we will struggle in vain to let it flow through us to our kids. But when his grace begins to transform our hearts, it also begins to transform our parenting. It's not about what we do. It's about what his grace does through us when we surrender to his wholehearted acceptance of us.

part 2

...

experiencing a vibrant friendship with Jesus

chapter 4
experiencing Jesus

And we all, who with unveiled faces contemplate the Lord's glory, are being transformed into his image with ever-increasing glory, which comes from the Lord, who is the Spirit.

—2 Corinthians 3:18

In my parents' front garden is a statue of Jesus sitting on a bench, holding two lambs in his arms. (Okay, so it's actually a statue of St. Francis, but you'll soon see why I'm calling it a statue of Jesus.) During a recent visit to my parents' house, this beautiful statue took on a whole new meaning to me.

The boys had been playing outside for much of the morning while my mom and I were sitting on the deck catching up. Only when Cal and Owen came running up to me for a glass of water did I realize that four-year-old Brennan was nowhere to be found. I searched the back yard and all throughout the house to no avail. Eventually I began calling Brennan's name for fear that he'd wandered off on his own.

Finally, Brennan came running into the house, shouting, "I'm right here, Mom!"

"Brennan," I asked, "where have you been, baby? I've been calling for you, and I was really starting to worry."

"Sorry, Mom!" He pointed in the direction of the statue of St. Francis. "I was out front playing with Jesus."

"Wow, baby," I said, a huge smile spreading across my face. "That is really wonderful. Did Jesus say anything to you while you were playing together?"

"Yep," Brennan replied. "He said, 'Thanks for playing with me!' Now can I go back outside?"

"Of course you can, sweetheart. Have fun!"

Experiencing Jesus

I'm inclined to believe that Brennan did indeed hear Jesus say those very words to him. What I do know for sure is that our children are learning that Jesus not only loves them but he also likes them! They are learning that Jesus wants to spend time with them, that he wants to be their Savior and their best friend.

It's a great and wonderful thing for our children to know about Jesus, but I'm increasingly convinced that Jesus' utmost desire is for them to actually experience him as their best friend. Of course we want our kids to understand that Jesus is completely holy and his greatness is far beyond our human comprehension — which actually makes the fact that he draws near to us even more astounding — but we also want them to know he is walking right beside them holding their hand.

Unfortunately we cannot make our children desire a friendship with Jesus. However, if I were being honest, I would admit that if I could, yes, I would make them love Jesus. But only because I have tasted his goodness and I don't want them to miss out on a single iota of it. The reality is our children will never come to love Jesus simply because that is what we want for them. "Let us keep looking to Jesus. Our faith comes from Him and He is the One Who makes it perfect" (Heb. 12:2 NLV). Our children will come to know and love Jesus only through their own experience of him. And this is the reason we plant seeds of faith in our children's hearts: that they might come to experience the goodness, and the greatness, and the faithfulness of Jesus Christ for themselves.

Tasting and Seeing

I have always loved Psalm 34:8: "Taste and see that the LORD is good." Only recently, however, God made the word *taste* practically jump off the page at me. His Spirit stirred in my heart and caused me to sit with this verse like I never had before. And in that moment, I became aware, anew, that God wants us to "taste" his goodness. Jesus longs for us to experience the fullness and the richness of his love for us, because only then can we let it flow through us as a love offering for Jesus to our children and the world. We cheat ourselves when we merely learn about it, debate it, or listen to others talk about their experience of it. Only when we actually "taste" it—experience it—shall we really know the joy that flows from being in a relationship with him.

Teaching our children how to experience the goodness of Jesus is at the core of leading them into a loving and vibrant friendship with him. But here is the catch. (Yes, I'm sorry, there is a catch.) "Taste and see" begins with us. Unfortunately, we get so wrapped up in the daily obligations of parenthood that we forego our own intimate encounters with God and neglect our own parched souls in the process.

Abiding in Jesus

Yes, taste and see begins with us because we cannot give what we have not received. If our own souls are thirsty, we will grow weary.

This is not about more *doing*. It's about *being*. Jesus invites us to come to him with our weary, worn-out, and burdened souls, not for a pep talk on how we can do more to make him more pleased but for rest. To just *be*: "Come to me, all you who are weary and burdened, and I will give you rest. Take my yoke upon you and learn from me, for I am gentle and humble in heart, and you will find rest for your souls. For my yoke is easy and my burden is light" (Matt. 11:28–30).

Jesus uses the imagery of the vine and the branches to teach us that to "be" is to remain or to abide in him. We must abide in him to bear the fruit of his love. "I am the vine; you are the branches. If you remain in me and I in you, you will bear much fruit; apart from me you can do nothing.... This is to my Father's glory, that you bear much fruit, showing yourselves to be my disciples" (John 15:5, 8).

> Jesus invites us to come to him with our weary, worn-out, and burdened souls and just *be*.

Rather than expect us to rely on our fragile strength and depleted resources, Jesus waters the soil of our souls so that we might bear the fruit of his love in the work we've been called to do. And in this case, the work we are talking about is parenting, the hardest but most rewarding work there is.

Indeed the practical responsibilities of parenting are hard work, but what I find infinitely harder than the day in and day out things that are required of me is being the *kind* of parent I desire to be. Having a loving, kind, patient, joyful, and thankful heart in the big *and* small stuff—now that's challenging!

Take the other day, for instance. It was a very difficult day at the end of an awful, terrible, no good, very bad week. While I was driving in the car on this particularly trying morning, an "unnamed child" was yelling at me from the back seat because his pants weren't tight enough, his shoelaces weren't tied correctly, his shirtsleeves were too long, and the sky was too blue. Gripping the steering wheel tightly while using up every last ounce of self-control left in my body, I begged, "Lord, you have got to change my son's heart!"

In that moment, these very words pierced the chaos swirling around in my head: "Jeannie, stop asking me to change your son's heart, and start asking how I want to change yours."

These gentle words of conviction invited me back into abiding, because the only way my heart can be changed and restored and renewed is if I am attached to "the vine." I have to abide.

Now, I'm afraid I know what you might be thinking right about now: "You have got to be kidding. Abide? I don't have time to rest! The only way I will get more rest is if I hire a babysitter more often, which means I'll feel guilty about spending more time away from my kids who need me. I can't rest. I have children to raise! I will abide later, but I don't have the luxury of abiding now!"

> The only way my heart can be changed and restored and renewed is if I am attached to "the vine."

I can assure you I had similar thoughts when I first began to learn about abiding. But here's the truth I had to face. If I want to give my children the best parts of me, I must allow God to do his good work within me. I must get quiet before the Lord and allow my soul the rest it craves. As we read in Isaiah 30:15, 18, "In repentance and rest is your salvation, in quietness and trust is your strength, but you would have none of it.... Yet the LORD longs to be gracious to you; therefore he will rise up to show you compassion." Dear Mom and Dad, are you worn out? Are you worried? Go to God. He *longs* to be gracious to you! He is with you in the trenches. He will show you compassion. Lean into him! "To live as God's child is to know, at this very instant, that you are loved by your Maker not because you try to please him and succeed, or fail to please him and apologize, but because he wants to be your Father. Nothing more. All your efforts to win his affection are unnecessary. All your fears of losing his affection are needless. You can no more make him want you than you can convince him to abandon you. ... You have a place at his table."[9]

Look, I know Jesus longs to answer my prayer, "Lord, less of me, more of you," but if I do not abide, my words return void. This is not because Christ is unfaithful—he remains so very faithful even in our unfaithfulness—but because we have to lean into him more and more to have a full tank from which to parent. I truly believe that in this process we become more of who Jesus created us to be as individuals, and therefore more of who we were created to be as parents for our children.

Drawing Close to God

A good starting place for identifying the ways in which you were uniquely created to abide is by asking yourself, "When do I feel closest to God? When do I most feel his presence in my life? When do I feel the most alive?" This is very different than just identifying times when you feel happy, and much more about the experiences that make you feel connected to God, the times when you can fill up on his love for you.

I draw close to God by worshiping to Christian music, meditating on Scripture, spending one-on-one time with friends or family who share my faith, and digging my toes into the sand while watching the waves crash along the shore. My husband would tell you that one of the ways he draws close to God is by running, whereas I run only when being chased. This is the beauty in abiding. Just as we are each uniquely created in the image of God, we each abide in our own unique way. And while abiding does require taking a time-out, it can also be integrated into everyday life by simply recognizing God's presence in the details. It is a process by which we become more purposeful in connecting intimately with God as we go throughout our day. Or as James puts it, "Come near to God and he will come near to you" (James 4:8).

Please don't hear this as something else you must do but as something he wants to do *for* you and *in* you. Come to him and *he* will give you rest. He will fill you up. All you have to do is have an open heart to receive his love for you.

Bearing Fruit

When we receive his love by remaining attached to the vine, our lives produce the fruit of the Spirit. Abiding in him equips us to "bear much fruit" even in the mundane responsibilities of parenthood. This is not to suggest that we will not have hard, sometimes painfully hard days, when all we want to do is run and hide where no small child can find us. *Of course we will have hard days.* Parenting, like life, will have its difficult days, trying weeks, and challenging seasons.

And because of these hard days in the adventure of parenting, we will not always feel happiness, because happiness is an emotion based on circumstances that are fleeting. We can, however, have joy and peace and hope, because joy, peace, and hope are based on the promises of Jesus. The joy of the Lord can be our strength when we grow weary (Neh. 8:10). His peace that passes all understanding can guard our hearts (Phil. 4:7), and our downcast souls can find hope in the faithfulness of his unfailing love (Ps. 43:5).

When I am feeling weary, I cling to Galatians 6:9: "Let us not become weary in doing good, for at the proper time we will reap a harvest if we do not give up." You might hear me walking around the house picking up the mess, putting the dishes away, folding laundry, disciplining and instructing (for the hundredth time today) while repeating, "Jesus, I am weary, but you are strong. I can't, but you can. Reap a harvest, Lord."

And while it's important to be honest about the fact that the Bible does not offer us any guarantees that we will see the harvest of his love in our kids' lives, I choose to walk in faith, faith being confidence in what we hope for and assurance about what we do not see (Heb. 11:1). Because I know the steadfastness of God's love and the power of his Word, I have faith that God will reap a harvest from the seeds we plant in our children's hearts, seeds that help them trust Jesus as their Savior and experience Jesus as their best friend.

Planting the Seed, Watching It Grow

Planting seeds of faith in our children's hearts begins with the interior work of teaching them who Jesus is and his loving acceptance of them, as we explored in the last chapter. Then, as our children begin to grasp their identity in Christ as "beloved children of God," they are more likely to become receptive to the other seeds we plant that nurture their friendship with him. Through seeds of faith, such as prayer, reading the Bible, Scripture memorization, worship, and service, we help our children experience Jesus in a way that enriches their knowledge of him and leads to a deeper relationship with him. Take a look at the following graph to see the cycle.

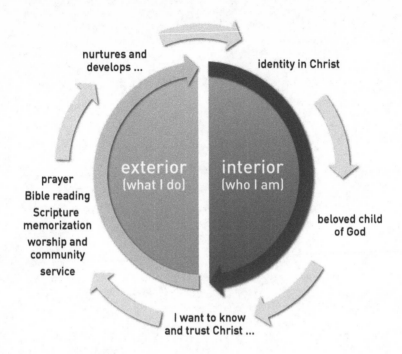

nurtures and develops ...

identity in Christ

exterior (what I do)

interior (who I am)

prayer
Bible reading
Scripture memorization
worship and community
service

beloved child of God

I want to know and trust Christ ...

Remember, these seeds of faith are not about checking "righteousness boxes" but about nurturing a trusting relationship with Jesus. Although it may be tempting to jump ahead to the how-tos of behavior modification — in other words, "How do I get my kids to obey and live a godly life?" — please don't! See, if we focus only on getting our kids to obey without first addressing the way grace and a relationship with Jesus inspire our hearts to grateful obedience, we'll end up creating law-abiding citizens on the outside but little rebels on the inside. And that little rebel won't stay captive forever.

Our children's desire to trust Jesus, grow in a vibrant friendship with him, and grow in Christlike character is nurtured through the seeds of faith we plant in their hearts and is empowered by his Spirit. Prayer, Bible reading, Scripture memorization, worship and community, and service all work together to unleash the Spirit's sanctifying power in their lives.

chapter 5

prayer

*Rejoice always, pray continually, give thanks
in all circumstances; for this is God's will
for you in Christ Jesus.*
—1 Thessalonians 5:16–18

I'm pretty sure that heaven is a little something like Palmetto Bluff, South Carolina. And well, if it's not, I may be a bit disappointed. There are no cars, no schedules, no stress. Only long afternoons at the pool overlooking the river, bike rides along beautiful winding roads, and bonfires with s'mores at sunset. It is the perfect family vacation, made for bonding.

For spring break last year, we decided it would be fun to drive, rather than fly as we usually do, to this little piece of heaven. This road trip was supposed to be a fourteen-hour drive, filled with fun, adventure, and excitement—something for us to reflect on with fond memories in the years to come. Instead, it was a twenty-one-hour road trip. Yes, twenty-one hours straight, starting with a projectile vomit by Owen so fierce it left us all breathing through our mouths for the remainder of the trip.

Our first day in the Bluff was bound to be a better day, and indeed it was. We set out on our bikes to explore the beautiful property. Brennan decided he wanted to ride on the back of my bike, Mike loaded up Owen on the back of his bike, Cal took off on his "look how fast I can go without training wheels now" bike, and off we went!

There is a reason they call the South God's Country, and Brennan was feeling the love. The same boy who loves to break-dance to songs like "Who Let the Dogs Out" is the same boy who burst into prayer while we were biking along the peaceful winding road in Palmetto Bluff. He prayed, "Dear Jesus, thank you for this beautiful day, thank you for the palm trees, thank you for my family, thank you for the pool. Aaaaa-men."

This beautiful boy of mine was inclined to pray his thankfulness. We are merely sowing the seed of prayer in the soil of his heart, but God, "who is able to do immeasurably more than all we ask or imagine, according to his power that is at work within us," is yielding the crop (Eph. 3:20).

Talking and Listening

Prayer is one of the earliest seeds of faith we can plant in our children's souls. One wonderful way to help our children understand prayer is to compare it to a relationship they have with a friend. We can explain that just as a relationship with a friend requires spending time together, talking to one another, and listening to each other, so does our relationship with Jesus. The purpose of the lesson is to help our children understand that one way we develop our friendship with Jesus is by talking *and* listening to him.

Praying words like "search me and know my heart" with our children teaches them to also engage in prayer as an opportunity to invite the Holy Spirit in to search their hearts and transform them into his image. Prayer is an awesome time to model for our kids just how much we need Jesus and to help them understand that prayer is not just a "help me, give me" speech (although at times those might be the only four words we have the faith or energy to muster up). Prayer is about growing into a deep and intimate relationship with Jesus, where we learn to trust him, recognize his Spirit leading us, and allow him to align our desires with his. Let us not take for granted our children's ability to listen to Jesus and be led by his Spirit in prayer. In fact, I often think that my children do a better job of listening to Jesus than I do.

Anywhere, Anytime, for Any Reason

I encourage you to pray *for* your children and to pray *with* your children—anywhere, anytime, and for any reason.

I first began to understand the significance of my prayers for my children through a wonderful book titled *Praying the Scriptures for Your Children* by Jodie Berndt. This book has been an extraordinary blessing in my prayer life because Jodie continually points us back to God's own words in Scripture and teaches us how to pray the steadfast promises of God over our children. She writes, "When you pray for your children, you join God in the work he is doing in their lives."[9] How amazing that God invites us to join him in the work he is doing in our kids' hearts, not through doing more and trying harder to make fewer mistakes but through the gift and the power of prayer. When we lay our kids before him and surrender our fears and worries, our weary mama souls can be filled with his peace, which passes all understanding. For "this is the confidence we

> God invites us to join him in the work he is doing in our kids' hearts through the gift and the power of prayer.

have in approaching God: that if we ask anything according to his will, he hears us. And if we know that he hears us—whatever we ask—we know that we have what we asked of him" (1 John 5:14–15).

What a gift we can give our kids by teaching them how to incorporate prayer into their life anywhere, anytime, and for any reason. And how important it is that we help our kids understand that prayer is not just for blessing the food or asking Jesus to keep us safe while we sleep. We can encourage our kids to pray before they start their day to ask Jesus for his blessing and guidance, when they sin or make a bad choice and they want to ask for forgiveness, when they feel happy or see something beautiful and they want to give thanks, when they need help controlling themselves and they need God's strength, or when they feel sad or scared and they need God's comfort. And we can teach our kids that sometimes prayer is simply, "Jesus, help!" as it often is for me in my most trying moments of parenting.

It is so essential that our children understand that there is no request too big, no feeling too bad, no shame too great, and no feeling too unworthy to express in prayer. We can come before our gracious Abba Father with honesty, with our struggles, and even with our doubts, and he will receive us with open arms. We must teach our children that prayer is not telling Jesus what we think he wants to hear, nor is it telling him anything he doesn't already know. Prayer is getting real with Jesus. We never have to fear his rejection. As Paul encourages us in James 1:5 (MSG), "If you don't know what you're doing, pray to the Father. He loves to help. You'll get his help, and won't be condescended to when you ask for it. Ask boldly, believingly, without a second thought."

One of the special ways we can engage our children in prayer is by starting the day asking how we can pray for each other. Before Daddy leaves for work, he asks the kids how he can pray for them that day, and the kids in turn ask Daddy how they can pray for him.

It's not only a wonderful way to get in touch with what's on each other's hearts every day but also a wonderful way to encourage one another in God's love. As we read in Psalm 5:3, "In the morning, Lord, you hear my voice; in the morning I lay my requests before you and wait expectantly."

One of the things we do to remind our children that we can pray anywhere and anytime is we take the prayer requests we just shared with each other and pray about them in the car on the way to school. I hope that by doing so my children learn that we can pray while buckled in our car seats just as easily as we can pray when we are all snuggled in our bunk beds at night. This is not to remove the sacredness of prayer or to negate the holiness of our awesome heavenly Father but to help our children understand that Jesus will listen to us anywhere and anytime.

> There is no request too big, no feeling too bad, no shame too great, and no feeling too unworthy to express in prayer.

It has been pretty awesome to watch our kids grow in their prayer lives. While Brennan and now Owen are typically the first ones to offer to proclaim their prayers aloud, I see the Spirit equally at work in Cal's heart. It's important to note that some children will tend to be more reserved in the way they pray aloud, and I do believe we have to honor this as a personality difference and not a receptivity difference. Jesus works in each of their little hearts in different ways, one not being better than another.

For example, when Cal was only four years old, I was supervising a play date he was having with a friend (whom we will call Ned) who was being unusually unkind. After several high drama instances, I noticed Cal close his eyes for a few moments. Unsure of what was wrong, I whispered in Cal's ear, "Honey, is everything okay?"

Cal opened his eyes and responded, "Mom, I was asking God to help Ned be kind to me."

When Mike got home that night, I told him how amazed I was by what Cal did. Little did I know that the previous night during bedtime, Mike had read a devotional with the kids about how we are to pray for those who are unkind to us.

Even Owen, while still developing his ability to put words to his thoughts, would participate in prayer by anticipating the amen. He would sit quietly through the prayer I'd whisper in his ear each night, and when I would come to the end and say, "In Jesus' precious and holy name we pray," I'd pause for Owen's amen. While he may have no understanding of the words I pray over him, he is indeed being blessed when he closes us in prayer. I can only imagine the joy of the Father, as his precious child proclaims, "Amen."

ACTS

A helpful resource for teaching children how to pray is the classic ACTS model of prayer:

- A: adoration
- C: confession
- T: thanksgiving
- S: supplication

If praying aloud with your children is fairly new to you, or if you are simply looking for new and creative ways to engage your children in prayer, you may want to consider the ACTS model. And if the words *adoration, confession, thanksgiving,* and *supplication* don't resonate with your children, you may want to substitute *wow, I'm sorry, thank you,* and *please.*

Below I offer just a few of the things we might say together in the ACTS model of prayer. Parents can lead, and children can follow.

Just remember to always allow your children an opportunity to say what's on their heart after you have led them through a portion of the prayer. In due time, they will be able to lead you!

Adoration (Wow)

We adore Jesus for who he is and what he has done for us. (He is God who has created us, Christ who has redeemed us, and the Holy Spirit who comforts us.) God our Creator sent his only Son, Jesus, who lived a perfect life, died on the cross, and rose again so that we may have abundant, forgiven life on earth, and eternal life in heaven with him. How special our children are to God that he would do that for them; we want them to own that!

A few ways we can adore him in prayer with our children include:

Lord, you are so awesome. You are worthy of our praise. You are amazing. You are powerful. You are perfect. You are more love than my heart can understand. Your grace is greater than I can fathom or comprehend. There is none like you. You are my Creator, my Abba Father, my Savior, and my best friend. I adore you, Jesus.

Give your child an opportunity to tell Jesus how awesome he is.

Confession (I'm sorry)

We confess our sin, our wrongdoings, and we accept his forgiveness that flows freely and generously.

One of the ways we can confess our sin to him in prayer with our children is inspired from the beautiful words in a prayer of confession from the 1979 Episcopal Book of Common Prayer. I have modified it below to make it more applicable to children.

Lord, we confess that we have sinned against you with our words, our thoughts, and our actions. We are sorry for the things we should have done and did not do, and for the things we did do but should not have done. Thank you that you know the depths of our hearts and our sin, but because of Jesus, you love us no matter what. Thank you for always forgiving us.

Thank you for loving to forgive us. Thank you for being our perfection and covering us with your righteousness.

Give your children an opportunity to confess words, thoughts, or actions to Jesus and to receive his forgiveness.

Thanksgiving (Thank you)

We thank Jesus for who we are in him and for everything he has given us. Our thankfulness is rooted in the recognition that everything we are and everything we have is a gift from God.

A few of the ways we can thank him in prayer with our children include:

Lord, thank you for making me so special. Thank you for making us a family. Thank you for loving me so much that you conquered death on the cross to have a friendship with me and to give me eternal life with you. Thank you for always being there for me. Thank you for hearing our prayers whenever we call on your name. Thank you for providing for all of our needs. Thank you for your grace! Thank you that your love for me never changes. I am so happy to know that on my best days of behavior and my worst days of behavior your love for me never changes; it is unconditional! Thank you for giving me your Spirit to guide me and comfort me. Thank you for loving me that much.

Give your children an opportunity to tell Jesus the things they are thankful for: people, experiences, feelings, his love, and so on. The list is endless.

Supplication (Please)

We present our requests to God and trust that his response (whatever it may be) will be rooted in his unconditional love for us, and we receive his peace.

A few of the ways we can present our requests to God in prayer with our children include:

Lord, please live your perfectly righteous life through us today. Help us love what you love and do what you'd do. Help us to be your love and light in this world. Please help me to be the awesome child that you created me to be. Please bless our family and loved ones. Please put your angels around us and protect us from fear and harm. Help us to trust you and rely on you today. Please help us see you in the details of our day and open our eyes to those we can love and serve with your heart. Please grant us your peace that passes all understanding and help us to know more of you today. Help us rest in your grace.

Give your children an opportunity to present their requests for help, healing, fears, and blessing and to receive his peace that passes all understanding.

In Jesus' precious and holy name we pray, amen!

The Lord's Prayer

Another wonderful way to pray with our children is through the Lord's Prayer. It is never too early to teach our children to pray how Jesus taught his disciples to pray in the gospel of Matthew — through the Lord's Prayer. Jesus himself said, "This, then, is how you should pray," and he gave us a model for prayer that begins with the precious word *Father*. "Our Father in heaven, hallowed be your name, your kingdom come, your will be done, on earth as it is in heaven. Give us today our daily bread. And forgive us our debts, as we also have forgiven our debtors. And lead us not into temptation, but deliver us from the evil one" (Matt. 6:9–13).

The Message translation of the Lord's Prayer is also worth noting here. While it may not be the version you recite on Sunday morning in church, it does offer a fresh perspective: "Our Father in heaven, Reveal who you are. Set the world right; Do what's best — as above, so below. Keep us alive with three square meals. Keep us forgiven with you and forgiving others. Keep us safe from ourselves and the

Devil. You're in charge! You can do anything you want! You're ablaze in beauty! Yes. Yes. Yes."

While the Lord's Prayer may not make much sense to our children because the words seem too lofty or obscure, we know that even at a young age it is meaningful for them to learn these prayers and begin to understand their power.

> We are invited to come before our great high King as his beloved sons and daughters and call him Abba, Daddy.

For example, notice the very precise way Jesus begins the Lord's Prayer with the word *Father*. *Abba* is the Aramaic word Jesus used for *Father*, an informal name we would often translate in the English language as *Daddy*.

Think about that for a moment. We can teach our children that we are invited to come before our Great High King as his beloved sons and daughters and call him Abba, Daddy.

I adore the way Sally Lloyd-Jones translates the Lord's Prayer in *The Jesus Storybook Bible*. It's such a precious way for our children to learn about praying as Jesus taught us to pray.

> Hello, Daddy!
> We want to know you and be close to you.
> Please show us how.
> Make everything in the world right again.
> And in our hearts, too.
> Do what is best—just like you do in heaven.
> And please do it down here too.
> Please give us everything we need today.
> Forgive us for doing wrong, for hurting you.
> Forgive us just as we forgive other people when they hurt us.
> Rescue us! We need you.
> We don't want to keep running away and hiding from you.

Keep us safe from our enemies.
You're strong, God. You can do whatever you want.
You are in charge. Now and forever and for always!
We think you're great!
Amen![10]

Jesus longs for us to bring everything (yes, everything) before him in prayer so that his peace, which far surpasses all human understanding, might flood our hearts and minds. There is no greater gift than the ability to go to Jesus with all things in prayer. As one of my favorite hymns testifies, "What a friend we have in Jesus, all our sins and grief to bear. What a privilege to carry everything to God in prayer. Oh, what peace we often forfeit, oh what needless pain we bear, all because we do not carry everything to God in prayer."

Play "Where Did You Experience God's Presence Today?"

If your children resist verbalizing their prayers, or if they resist prayer altogether, one fun way to normalize prayer and nurture your child's friendship with Jesus is through a game we play at night called "Where did you experience God's presence today?" It's a slight knock-off from the "high and low" game you may be aware of.

First we ask, "What was your 'high' today?" What made you really happy or what brought you joy?

Next we ask, "What was your 'low' today?" What made you sad or hurt your feelings? While my kids initially resisted the invitation to talk about the things that made them sad (they said they didn't want to think about it), I believe it's important for parents to know and speak into the places where our children struggle, whether it be in academics, friendships, or self-worth.

And finally, we ask, "Where did you experience God's presence today?" Did someone say or do something kind? Did you feel comforted or protected? Did you see something beautiful or awesome? Did he speak to you or nudge your spirit when you had to make a choice? Did someone make you feel really loved? The list goes on, but the point is simple: God is in the details, desiring your attention, longing to reveal himself to you and pour love and peace into your heart. So keep your eyes open for him! This game transitions into a prayer as we close it with, "God, we thank you for the highs and we thank you for the lows. We thank you that you are with us in both."

As Paul reminds us: "Don't worry about anything; instead, pray about everything. Tell God what you need, and thank him for all he has done. Then you will experience God's peace, which exceeds anything we can understand. His peace will guard your hearts and minds as you live in Christ Jesus" (Phil. 4:6–7 NLT).

chapter 6
Bible reading

Faith comes from hearing the message,
and the message is heard through the
word about Christ.

—Romans 10:17

Last year, on one of the first beautiful days of summer, I packed up the cooler and took all three children to the beach. We arrived with our beach toys, shovels, and fishing nets. While I focused on making sure Owen didn't drown in the ocean, which he was desperately trying to do, Cal found a group of friends and quickly joined in the quest to build the best sand castle on the beach. Brennan, however, ran straight for the water's edge, began throwing heaps of sand into the ocean, flexing his little muscles, and yelling, "Take that, you Philistines—I will defeat you!"

While I'm sure some people were looking at Brennan like he'd gone mad, I couldn't have been more thrilled. Brennan was pretending to be David defeating the Philistines in God's strength. He was acting out his favorite story in the Bible, the story of a young boy who became an unlikely hero when he fought and defeated the seemingly undefeatable giant Goliath—a story in the Old Testament that sets the stage for another, greater hero (Jesus) who would soon come to defeat an even bigger giant (sin and death). Indeed, God's powerful Word can penetrate tender little hearts.

How Do We Approach the Bible?

Hillsong Kids has an awesome song called "Jesus Is My Superhero!" Many years ago, when my children started becoming interested in superheroes and action figures, this very song got me wondering about how I could help our children get just as excited about our holy, awesome, and powerful God as they get about pretending to be Superman or Spider-Man defeating the villains.

My approach to this started with assessing how I approach the Bible with my kids. Oh how important it is that I remember that God's Word is not primarily about me and what I should be doing but about God and what he has already done through Christ Jesus. Reading the Bible through that lens changes everything. And I do believe our own attitude about the Bible has a huge impact on our kids' desire to read Scripture.

See the difference in these two scenarios:

- *Scenario 1:* "Okay, kids, pick two fun books off the shelf, but then we have to read a Bible story too. You can't go to bed before you read the Holy Bible, because you have to learn about Jesus so you can try hard to be like him. You will read it and you will like it!"
- *Scenario 2:* "Okay, kids, choose one book off the shelf and then choose one Bible story. I can't wait to see how Jesus will reveal himself to us tonight through his awesome Word. I love reading about what God did for us and how much he loves us!"

See, approaching the Bible with great expectancy that Jesus will meet us there is the first step in getting our kids just as excited about learning about Christ and his followers as they get about Superman, Transformers, Barbie, and Dora. Perhaps you might even find your kids wanting to imitate Jesus and his followers as much as they want to imitate the heroes, princesses, and villains that our culture celebrates.

Growing Our Trust

My three-year-old son, Owen, stood by the side of the pool, pondering whether he trusted his daddy enough to jump into his arms in the shallow end of the pool. Owen knows his daddy loves him. He knows his daddy provides for him. He even knows how much his daddy enjoys him. But does he know he can trust his daddy enough to jump into his arms in a place where his only hope is his daddy's catching him?

As Owen pondered what to do, my husband said things like, "Owen. It's okay, buddy. Don't be afraid. You can trust Daddy. Jump into my arms. I love you, and I promise I'll catch you." As Owen listened, I saw his courage increase. His heart was softening. His guard was coming down. His trust was growing. He was slowly moving toward the edge of the pool, toes now dangling over the side, preparing to jump into his father's arms.

As I watched this scenario play out, I was reminded that reading the Bible does to my own soul what my husband's words were doing to my son's soul. As I meditate on God's Word, my courage increases, my heart softens, my guard comes down, and *my trust grows*.

When I am on the side of the pool, desiring to surrender my fear and doubt for the courage to jump, to trust in God, I run to his Word. There I find my heavenly Father saying, "Don't be afraid. You can trust your Father. Jump into my arms. I love you, and I promise I will catch you." And as I learn to trust him in the shallow end of the pool, I become willing to go a little farther into the deep end of trust, where I really begin to experience his unfailing faithfulness to me.

Not only do we find our trust and hope when we read the Bible but also we find direction and purpose. As Psalm 119:105 says, "Your word is a lamp for my feet, a light on my path." God speaks to us through his infallible Word, providing a strong foundation for our stumbling feet and a lit path back home for our wandering hearts.

• • • • • • • • • • • • • • • • •

As I meditate on God's Word, my courage increases, my heart softens, my guard comes down, and _my trust grows._

• • • • • • • • • • • • • • • •

When our children are young, we can read Scripture aloud to them. This is something my husband and I aim to do with our children every night at bedtime. (*Aim* being the key word!) We open God's Word and let our hearts and minds be filled with his glory (or, as we tell our kids, with his awesomeness). And as our kids get older and learn to read on their own, we can also encourage them to spend time alone in God's Word, reading his love letter to them.

For example, our oldest son, Cal, is now eight years old and has several Bibles from which to choose. He is truly learning that the Bible is a book our hearts never tire of. It's not unusual for him to choose to read the Bible just as quickly as he chooses a book he checked out from the library. God's Word does that; it captivates us as we let it seep into our souls.

Using Children's Story Bibles

A key element in engaging our younger children in Scripture reading is using a children's Bible to which they can relate. The stories in children's Bibles are no less incredible and truthful than those in an adult's Bible; they are just written in a way that speaks to little hearts, and the stories have pictures that keep our children's attention.

There are many excellent children's Bibles to choose from, including *The Jesus Storybook Bible* by Sally Lloyd-Jones and *The Big Picture Story Bible* by David Helm. Our youngest ones can snuggle up with God's Word using Bibles such as Sally Lloyd-Jones's *Baby's Hug-a-Bible*. The *Kids' Devotional Bible*, which has devotions scattered throughout the text, is a good Bible geared toward school-aged children. Each of these Bibles does a wonderful job of bringing God's Word to life for our children in an honest, exciting, and age-appropriate way.

In *The Jesus Storybook Bible*, Sally Lloyd-Jones reminds us that we should resist the temptation to reduce the Bible to a series of morality tales or lists of dos and don'ts and encourages us to teach our children about the Bible in this wonderful way:

> Now some people think the Bible is a book of rules, telling what you should and shouldn't do. The Bible certainly does have some rules in it. They show you how life works best. But the Bible isn't mainly about you and what you should be doing. It's about God and what He has done. Other people think the Bible is a book of heroes, showing you people you should copy. The Bible does have some heroes in it, but ... most of the people in the Bible aren't heroes at all. They make some big mistakes (sometimes on purpose), they get afraid and run away. At times they are downright mean. No, the Bible isn't a book of rules, or a book of heroes. The Bible is most of all a Story. It's an adventure story about a young Hero who comes from a far country to win back his lost treasure. It's a love story about a brave Prince who leaves his palace, his throne—everything—to rescue the one he loves. It's like the most wonderful of fairy tales that come true in real life. You see, the best thing about this Story is—it's true! There are lots of stories in the Bible, but all the stories are telling one Big Story. The Story of how God loves his children and comes to rescue them.[11]

It is *never* too early to start reading the Bible with your children. Learning God's Word is one of the ways our children come to know the heart of God. Their brains are little sponges, waiting to absorb the truths about God's great love for them. These stories teach our children that the Creator of the universe made them and loves them and is intimately involved in every detail of their lives. They reveal God's faithfulness, his greatness, his goodness, and his grace. They remind our children that there is no detail too big or too small for our God. And most wonderfully, all of these stories point our children to the one great story woven from the very first to the very last sentence in the Bible—the story of our Savior, Jesus Christ, and his life, death, resurrection, ascension, and his coming again.

While our young children cannot fully appreciate *all* the story has to offer, we must trust the story and the power of God's Word. We are planting the seeds and the story will grow in meaning for them as they grow in their understanding of the gospel.

Allowing Hard Questions

I want to acknowledge a hard truth. As you may well know, reading the Bible can spark our children's minds and hearts, and lead them to ask some pretty wise (and tough!) questions too. And when this happens, it's easy to get nervous and either pretend we know more than we do or simply avoid the conversation with a distraction. I want to encourage you to be vulnerable with your kids in this area. Allow them to ask hard questions. You don't have to be afraid to acknowledge that you don't have all the answers and that there are so many things about God, and the Bible, that will remain a mystery until we see him face to face (Rom. 11:33–36; 1 John 3:2–3).

Allowing our children to explore their faith and the things that don't always make sense teaches our children to bring those questions to us instead of burying them where doubt can pile up. In fact, we can use our children's questions as opportunities to teach them about what the Bible says about faith: "Now faith is confidence in what we hope for and assurance about what we do not see" (Heb. 11:1). And we can help them uncover the thrill of coming to trust

Jesus and encountering him in our curiosity, even when life doesn't seem to make sense. He meets us even in our doubt and lack of trust. He can handle it! And he can fill our empty wells of disbelief with living waters of belief through the power of his Spirit at work within us (1 Cor. 2:6–16). He empowers us to respond to his love through the gift of his Holy Spirit.

That being said, there are many questions about God and the Bible that have clear answers, and a wonderful resource for exploring our kids' questions about the Bible is *If I Could Ask God Anything* by Kathryn Slattery. And while Slattery's book does a great job of tackling "toughies," ultimately it encourages young hearts to embrace a personal relationship with God through faith in Jesus Christ.

Finally, and perhaps most important, when your children ask tough questions, ask God for wisdom. As we read in James 1:5, "If any of you lacks wisdom, you should ask God, who gives generously to all without finding fault, and it will be given to you." Often, when my boys ask questions to which I do not have an immediate answer, I affirm their desire to know and understand the Scriptures, I tell them Mommy will ask God for wisdom to answer their questions, and I remind them that the one thing I know beyond a shadow of a doubt is that Jesus is downright crazy about them.

> When your children ask tough questions, ask God for wisdom.

Resources beyond the Bible

Devotionals, videos, music, and children's books are just some of the other wonderful resources we can integrate into our daily lives to nurture our children's knowledge of and friendship with Jesus. Some are gender specific, while others are age specific.

Children's devotionals are a great way to begin the day as a family in God's Word. Our family begins the day with the wondrous *Thoughts to Make Your Heart Sing* by Sally Lloyd-Jones. Though described as a devotional for six- to nine-year-old children, I also find my spirit fed by the inspiring words on each page. I would recommend this devotional to children and parents of *all* ages. And *Blessings Every Day* by Carla Barnhill is a good devotional for the very young. Starting our day in God's Word is how we write his Word on our hearts and fill up our tanks with his love.

As far as videos go, I'm thrilled with the content in the latest video series by Phil Vischer, creator of Veggie Tales, called *What's in the Bible?* I highly commend these to you. Not only do our kids enjoy these videos but also they are learning about the grace of God in the Old and New Testaments.

Christian music is also an awesome way to draw our kids' hearts and minds into a place of worship and to write God's Word on their hearts. Few things bring me more joy than listening to my kids singing along to worship music in our kitchen or in the back seat of the car. It's in these precious moments that I'm reminded of what the Lord says in Isaiah 55:11, "My word that goes out from my mouth: It will not return to me empty, but will accomplish what I desire and achieve the purpose for which I sent it."

When we pour God's Word into our kids' hearts, it's sure to pour out.

(For more recommendations of age-appropriate Bibles, devotionals, books, videos, and songs that will nurture your child's faith, visit *www.jeanniecunnion.com/resources.*)

chapter 7
Scripture memorization

I seek you with all my heart; do not let me
stray from your commands. I have hidden
your word in my heart that I might not sin
against you. Praise be to you, LORD;
teach me your decrees.

—Psalm 119:10–12

At last they arrived—the beautiful ABC Scripture memory cards I'd been waiting for. I was so excited to get my hands on these cards and begin thinking about the different ways in which we could use them in our home to memorize Scripture as a family. On the night they arrived, I explained to the kids that we were going to read through each of the Scripture cards and choose a few to begin memorizing. "These cards are going to help us hide God's Word in our hearts!" I said with a big smile.

Brennan furrowed his brow. "But Mom, if I hide God's Word in my heart, doesn't that mean I can't share it with others? I thought we were supposed to share God's Word."

Oh, how I love the questions they ask. So I gave my best shot at explaining to Brennan that hiding God's Word in our hearts is a lot like writing his Word on our hearts with a permanent marker. And in the days and weeks that followed his question, I devoted myself to helping Brennan (and Cal and Owen) understand some of the wonderful things that happen when we write God's Word on our hearts. Things like:

- We have immediate access to the love and hope and comfort that his Word provides.
- We are empowered to fight sin.
- We are equipped to let the light of Christ shine through our words, for the glory of God.

But before we explore these benefits further, we must start by remembering that Scripture memorization, like all structured spiritual practices, is not about obedience to the practice itself. And the purpose of Scripture memorization is not to put another notch in our holy belt so that self-righteousness and dry religion can take root. Rather, Scripture memorization helps keep our hearts intricately woven with God's. We hide his Word in *our* hearts so that we may stay close to *his* heart.

Now, let's get back to a few of the benefits of Scripture memory that we can teach our children. Through memorized Scripture, we have immediate access to the love and hope and comfort that his Word provides. And this hope is not meant to be written on our hearts to be savored alone; it's meant to be shared for the nourishment of those we encounter (including our kids) who need a fresh dose of godly encouragement.

See, I think Scripture memorization is often thought of as merely a tool for training and instructing our children in righteousness. And yes, while that is a wonderful benefit we will explore here in a minute, I want to start by acknowledging the power of Scripture to affirm our kids in God's wholehearted and unconditional love for them in Jesus Christ. Yes, we can flood our children's hearts with his love by teaching them to memorize Scripture about their identity in Christ as beloved children of God. God didn't give us his written Word merely to convict and instruct us. What a tragedy to think of the Bible that way. God gave us his written Word to express his unconditional love for us, to reveal himself to us, to redeem and restore us through his grace and forgiveness. The Bible is, in essence, his love letter to us. And on most days, I need this love letter more for myself than I need it for use in parenting my children, because it reminds me that God is in control and his grace is, well, simply extravagant.

For example, on a morning when I open my eyes to what feels like pure hopelessness before the day has even begun, I recite from memory, over and over again, until it finds its way deep into my soul, Psalm 42:11 (NLT): "Why am I discouraged? Why is my heart so sad? I will put my hope in God! I will praise him again—my Savior and my God!" Or on a day when one of my children is experiencing sadness or defeat, I hold him close and recite in his ear Psalm 34:18 (NLT): "The Lord is close to the brokenhearted; he rescues those whose spirits are crushed." I do this because when we quote Scripture, our words carry the full power of God's Word (Isa. 55:11).

> When we quote Scripture, our words carry the full power of God's Word.

Second, during times of Scripture memory, we can teach our children how "the word of God is alive and powerful" (Heb. 4:12 NLT) and empowers us to fight sin. As Paul told Timothy, "All Scripture is inspired by God and is useful to teach us what is true and to make us realize what is wrong in our lives. It corrects us when we are wrong and teaches us to do what is right. God uses it to prepare and equip his people to do every good work" (2 Tim. 3:16–17 NLT).

One of several instances where Jesus demonstrates God's Word as "alive and powerful" is in Matthew 4. After Jesus fasted for forty days and forty nights, Satan confronted him in the desert with three opportunities to sin. It is important to note that Jesus' temptation was not merely symbolic. He was "tempted in every way, just as we are—yet he did not sin" (Heb. 4:15). And although Jesus was the Son of God, he defeated Satan by using a weapon that we all have at our disposal: "the sword of the Spirit, which is the word of God" (Eph. 6:17). Jesus met temptation with spiritual truth, with Scripture, and we can use his example to help our children see that the Word of God is alive and powerful in their lives too.

For example, when I see one of our boys struggling with self-control, I might encourage him to pray the words of Paul in Philippians 2:13: "God, please work in me, and give me the desire and the power to do what pleases you." Or when I see my son struggling with selfishness, I encourage him to pray the words of Philippians 2:3–5: "Lord, help me do nothing out of selfish ambition, but in humility, help me value others' interests above my own." Having these words written on their hearts with a permanent marker helps them defeat sin with the active and powerful Word of God.

And finally, we can teach our children how Scripture memorization equips us to let the light and love of Christ shine through our words, for the glory of God. In John 13:35 Jesus says, "By this everyone will know that you are my disciples, if you love one another." Love lived out for one another, *and* truth spoken in love, bears witness to Christ. As the apostle Peter instructs in 1 Peter 3:15 (NLT), "Your heart should be holy and set apart for the Lord God. Always be ready to tell everyone who asks you why you believe as you do. Be gentle as you speak and show respect." I love the quote attributed to St. Francis of Assisi: "Preach the gospel at all times, and when necessary, use words." And what words shall we use? The gospel of the grace of God.

Chuck Swindoll wrote this about the power of Scripture memorization: "I know of no other single practice in the Christian life more rewarding, practically speaking, than memorizing Scripture.... No other single exercise pays greater spiritual dividends! Your prayer life will be strengthened. Your witnessing will be sharper and much more effective. Your attitudes and outlook will begin to change. Your mind will become alert and observant. Your confidence and assurance will be enhanced. Your faith will be solidified."[12]

Of course not all of these reasons are relevant or practical for a young child, but in due time, they will be. Until then, when you memorize Scripture with your children, one of the practical ways you can help the verse become alive and powerful to them is to talk about how it can be applied in their lives. Some questions you can use to do this include:

- How does this verse reflect the character of God and his nature toward us?
- How does this verse teach us how we can grow in Christlikeness?
- How does this verse equip us to meet temptation with spiritual truth?
- What does this verse teach us about God's grace?

As Life Happens

A practical way to incorporate Scripture memory into everyday life is to impress God's truth on your children as "life happens." Moses taught us this principle when he instructed the Israelite people on what to do with the commandments he'd just given them: "These commandments that I give you today are to be on your hearts. Impress them on your children. Talk about them when you sit at home and when you walk along the road, when you lie down and when you get up" (Deut. 6:6–7).

For example, if you want to practice Scripture memorization with your kids, you might choose a new verse each week that you will recite together in the morning and in the evening so that by the end of the week you will have memorized a new verse. But reciting the verse doesn't have to be restricted to morning and evening. As you go about your day with your children, you can look for ways to incorporate the memory verse as "life happens," thus teaching your children how to incorporate it into daily life. To illustrate this point, I'd like to share a story with you.

> Impress God's truth on your children as "life happens."

The other morning, our boys were playing an intense game of basketball in the playroom. As usual, I heard the typical shenanigans that ensue when boys compete with one another. But on this particular occasion and to my great surprise, I also overheard Cal say to his brother, "Brennan, keep your tongue from evil!"

I was pretty sure my ears were playing tricks on me, so I hurried to the playroom to get the full story. "Hey, guys, what's going on in here?" I asked.

Cal was the first to reply. "Mom, Brennan was about to say something mean to me, so I reminded him to keep his tongue from evil."

Sure enough, Brennan immediately chimed in with, "And I stopped myself, and I didn't say anything unkind, Mom! Thanks for helping me, Cal!"

Cal knew this particular verse—"Keep your tongue from evil," found in Psalm 34:13—because we'd recently memorized it with the boys. Hearing Cal encourage his brother with this verse was pretty awesome. That being said, please know I'm not pretending this is a common occurrence in our home. Trust me, reciting Bible verses to one another is not how they typically react when offended by each other. This situation was, however, a simple reminder that God's Word is alive and powerful, and Scripture memorization does yield its fruit, even in young children. As the psalmist writes, "Blessed is the one ... whose delight is in the law of the LORD, and who meditates on his law day and night. That person is like a tree planted by streams of water, which yields its fruit in season and whose leaf does not wither—whatever they do prospers" (Ps. 1:1–3).

Cast a Vision with Life Verses

"Do you know you're part of God's great story?" That's a question we often like to ask our kids to cast a vision for why they were created and to lead them in the great story God has written for them. As David wrote, "You saw me before I was born. Every day of my life was recorded in your book. Every moment was laid out before a single day had passed" (Ps. 139:16 NLT).

The great narrative of Jesus' love and work in this world does not end at Jesus' ascension or at the end of Revelation. It continues in our own lives as we enact the great story of creation (birth), the fall (sin), redemption (our salvation), and sanctification (the ongoing process of growing in his likeness).

Therefore, Mike and I encourage our children to live in great expectation of what God has planned for them, as described in

> Do you know you're part of God's great story?

1 Corinthians 2:9 (NLT): "No eye has seen, no ear has heard, and no mind has imagined what God has prepared for those who love him." Our message to our children is, "He is *for* you. He has a purpose for your life! You are part of something greater than yourself." When we have to train and discipline and love our kids in hard ways, we often

remind them that part of our job, as their parents, is to direct them back to God's stream of grace. We want to help our kids catch the vision—to help them think about not only *what* they want to do when they grow up but, more important, *who* they want to be. We want them to think of their life story as being part of God's great story. So we gave each of them their very own life verse to memorize, a verse that begins the story God has written especially for them. Here is a little glimpse into how we chose life verses for each of them.

Cal's Verse

Twenty weeks into my pregnancy with Cal, Mike and I bounded into our sonogram appointment anxious to hear the news of whether our growing and thriving unborn baby would soon be wearing pink or blue. Sadly, what I originally thought would be one of the more thrilling moments in my life quickly turned grim. The technician doing the sonogram attempted to hide her angst (to no avail) as she told us we were having a boy but that she would need to get the doctor to talk to us a bit more about what she found. After what felt like an eternity, a stark man with zero bedside manner entered the room to inform us that there were a few "soft markers" that indicated our son could have Down syndrome. From that moment on, much of what the doctor said was a blur, but what I do remember with complete clarity were his piercing words: "You'll need to weigh your options and decide quickly if you want to continue with this pregnancy."

It was 4:00 p.m. on a Friday afternoon when we were handed this potentially life-altering news and told to "sit tight" until Monday when we could talk to a genetic specialist about our options. Mike and I walked back to our apartment in a haze having no idea what our future held, but what we did know, beyond a shadow of a doubt, was that our son, this precious little life, was ours. For better or worse, in sickness and in health, he was our son, and there were no options to consider or new decisions to be made. The sorrow was deep and wide that night, but I assured my son, as I whispered to my belly, that he was safe and sound, and he was loved. And then I committed my every waking moment to praying for healing, protection, and blessing over his developing life.

Not long after we were given this news, Mike and I decided to take a weekend retreat to California to rest and pray and reflect. Within hours of arriving at the resort, Mike took off for his usual daily run. And on this particular day, I did something I don't usually do—I went for a little jog myself. (Okay, so maybe it was more like a fast walk.)

As I walked up the side of the mountain on the most beautiful oceanside trail I've ever experienced, listening to Christian music on my iPod, and praying for protection over Cal's little life, the words in Psalm 139 started bouncing around in my brain. This is one of those passages I already knew well, because I had memorized it in years past. But now more than ever, I could appreciate the words in the psalm, and it became the one I prayed countless times during my pregnancy: "I praise you because I am fearfully and wonderfully made; your works are wonderful, I know that full well" (Ps. 139:14).

Many months later Cal was born perfectly healthy, but in those countless hours of prayer, I was given God's peace that passes all understanding. I was reminded that no matter what special needs Cal might have, our son would be perfectly created in God's image, and I would love him with every ounce of my being. And so Cal's life verse became Psalm 139:14.

Brennan's Verse

When Cal turned one, I basically "let God know" that we'd decided we were ready for another child. Unsurprisingly, God didn't need me to let him know anything other than "Lord, your will be done." There were many months of disappointing negative pregnancy tests and countless hours of pleading with God to give us exactly what we wanted, exactly when we wanted it (ridiculous, I know). Rest assured, I did my very best to control and manipulate the situation.

My moment of surrender came while watching a Beth Moore video. Something Beth said in her video (although her exact words I cannot recall) opened up my heart just enough to let these precise words flood my soul: "Jeannie, I am being selfish with you right now. We have some time to spend together first." I knew with utter certainty the source of those words, and my heart was overcome with peace.

I surrendered to the outrageous thought that Jesus loved me so much that he was more interested in the work he wanted to do in me and with me than he was concerned with giving me exactly what I thought I wanted at the very moment I thought I wanted it. And ultimately, the desire of my heart for another child made me tender to his Spirit, his leading, and yes, even his timing.

During the waiting, I began journaling Scripture about God's great love for me, and I found comfort in the verses that spoke of me as his child. One particular verse, 1 John 3:1, resonated within me: "See what great love the Father has lavished on us, that we should be called children of God!" This verse carried me through the waiting. One year later, when we found out we were pregnant once again, we knew we would give this life verse to Brennan, our second son, as a beautiful reminder that Jesus loved him, as his child, infinitely more than we could fathom.

Owen's Verse

Owen's story was significantly less dramatic but all the same wonderful. Soon after Mike and I talked about adding another child to our family, we found out I was pregnant with Owen. Staring at that little stick that said +, I was overcome with gratitude. As I sat on the edge of our bed, crying happy tears and thanking God for giving us another child, one of my favorite hymns came to mind: "Bless the Lord, O my soul, and all that is within me, bless his holy name. He has done great things."

I could not remember where the verse (from which the hymn originated) was in the Bible, but I did know I was just given the life verse I would use for our third child. I pulled myself together, grabbed my Bible, looked up the verse in the concordance, and found what I was looking for: "Let all that I am praise the LORD; with my whole heart, I will praise his holy name. Let all that I am praise the LORD; may I never forget the good things he does for me" (Ps. 103:1–2 NLT).

The words "Let all that I am" in Psalm 103 refer to our soul. However, in that moment, all I could think was that "all that I am" meant my physical body, where Owen's precious little life was being formed. Acknowledging my joy, God had given me the verse to celebrate and give thanks for the great things he had done in giving us this child. And our third son, Owen, had his life verse.

● ● ●

Watching our boys come to understand how their stories began and why we chose the verses we did has been a beautiful thing. Through memorizing life verses, we can teach our children to seek God and his Word first, and trust him to reveal the purpose for which they were so wonderfully created. As the Lord declares in Jeremiah 29:11–13, "For I know the plans I have for you, plans to prosper you and not to harm you, plans to give you hope and a future. Then you will call on me and come and pray to me, and I will listen to you. You will seek me and find me when you seek me with all your heart."

(For more wonderful Scripture memorization resources, visit *www.jeanniecunnion.com/resources*.)

My friend Annesley, who has three boys much older than mine, once gave me beautiful advice about Scripture memorization. She explained, "When my children would ask me what I wanted for my birthday, every year I would tell them the same thing: 'Please, don't buy me something. Instead, pick a Bible verse, memorize it, and recite it to me on my birthday. Writing God's Word on your hearts is the best gift you could give me.'" Later, as I reflected on her wise words, the profound meaning behind her message hit me: one sure way to open your children's hearts to loving Scripture is for them to first see how much you love it.

chapter 8

worship
and community

I rejoiced with those who said to me,
"Let us go to the house of the LORD."
—Psalm 122:1

Chaos, challenge, fatigue. Do any of these words characterize your Sunday mornings like they do many of ours? I often wonder when walking into church, "Were heads spinning, voices rising, and shoes flying as they shoved one another into the car this morning? How many other families here are smiling on the outside but still recovering on the inside from the way their Sunday morning began?" Of course, not all of our Sunday mornings are that hard, but some certainly are. This is real life, people, and real life can be ugly. Although getting to church may not be easy, it's important, vitally important, to worship in community.

Why Worship in Community Matters

When we make worship a priority, we give our children the opportunity to see their parents, and others, worshiping Jesus in community. In doing so, we teach them the value of making space and time as a family to worship. We affirm our commitment to put Christ at the center of our family not just in word but also in action.

In their book *Sticky Faith*, Kara Powell and Chap Clark do a wonderful job of exploring the importance of Christian community in our children's lives, especially as they get older. They write:

> As we planned our College Transition Project, the Fuller Youth Institute research team had hoped to find one thing that parents and church leaders could do that would be the silver bullet of Sticky Faith. We had hoped to find one element of kids' church involvement that would be significantly related to higher faith maturity — head and shoulders above the rest.
>
> We haven't found that silver bullet. While the study of Scripture, small groups, mentoring, retreats, justice work, and a host of other ministry activities are important, the reality is that kids' spiritual growth is far more complicated than just one silver bullet.
>
> The closest our research has come to that definitive silver bullet is this sticky finding: for high school and college students, there is a relationship between attendance at church-wide worship services and Sticky Faith.[13]

Worship in community matters!

The Purpose of Churchwide Worship

Too often people think of church as the place where happy people go to get happier. Or worse, the place where Christians who are pretending to be happy go to pretend to be happier. Both couldn't be farther from the truth.

If and only if you are worshiping in a church that preaches the gospel of *good news* — the gospel of grace — will you find your heart convicted, set free, transformed, and renewed through worship. And for the sake of your children, I urge you to find a community that gives your kids this grace. Find a church that demonstrates the greatness and goodness of Christ to your kids and introduces them to the faith experience as an awesome adventure, not a deadly bore. Find a church that teaches that being a Christian is grounded not in what you can do for Jesus but in what Jesus has already done for you.

I'm on my soapbox, but this topic is important. I was reminded just how important it is when a dear woman of faith asked this question on my website: "How do we get our young kids excited about church? Every single Sunday I have to deal with a pouty face and a bad attitude. I don't know how to instill in him the joy of worship."

Many children fight going to church and leave the church the second they are set free to make their own choices. They leave because they experience church as a place where you go to be condemned, preached at, and sent on your way to do more, try harder, and do better at making God happy with you. So many of our churches are laying burden after burden on our children either by giving them unachievable to-do lists for living a perfectly blissful life now or by telling them their worth before God and his acceptance of them are based on how they are performing in their daily lives. Oh, how I believe this grieves the heart of our heavenly Father. Please find a church that gives your kids grace. It's one of the greatest gifts you can give them.

Now, I'm not suggesting you go in search of the perfect church, for there isn't such a thing. Imperfect people cannot create a

> Imperfect people cannot create a perfect church. We can only worship a perfect God.

perfect church. We can only worship a perfect God. No, what I am saying and what's so important for our children to understand is this: church is the place where broken people go to be with other broken people, to fall at the mercy and grace of our Lord Jesus Christ and to be filled afresh with his love. Church is where we bring our sadness and suffering *and* our thankfulness and joy. This is church and this is community as Christ intended it. We were created to be in community and fellowship with one another, to confess our brokenness and our need for a Savior, to celebrate the divine exchange of our sin for his perfect righteousness, and to worship in awe and wonder with forgiven and grateful hearts.

Learning to Love Worship

Let's say your church does preach a gospel of grace but still your child complains. What should you do then? How can you help your child develop a love of worship? Before you come down hard on your child for his pouty face and negative attitude toward church, look for what might be causing that attitude, and then work to address it.

As in every other area of parenting, start by examining yourself. Are you approaching worship with your children as a joy? Do you present church as something you *have* to do or something you, praise God, *get* to do? Do you love to snuggle with your kids in the pew, or exchange a smile with them as you are raising your voices together in song? Or are you constantly frowning, correcting, and shushing?

Then let's look at your children. Are they too small and wiggly to sit still for a long time? Do you attend a church that has a separate children's program, where they can play, sing, and hear Bible stories during the adult sermon? Or have you considered giving your children a special notebook and markers to doodle, draw, and reflect on the words they hear?

We must remember, we cannot make our children desire to worship Jesus any more than we can make them fall in love with him. If this is a battle in your home, begin and end the battle with prayer. Don't lose hope. Seek to understand your child's hesitation. Listen.

Encourage. Share with your child the reasons you desire to worship. And remember, just because your child does not want to attend church today does not mean your child will not want to attend church tomorrow. The fruit of grace is almost always in the future. Endure with the prayer that their hearts will melt under the fire of his love. And keep worshiping!

Worship Changes Us

We worship because it changes us. Have you ever noticed that? How making the choice to worship in song, in sacrament, in receiving, and in giving changes us? It's one of the beautiful reasons God calls us to do it—to be changed. God doesn't need our worship. He does indeed delight in it and is glorified through it, but he doesn't need it. We, the fallen and broken, need it because worship changes us. Worship can take our eyes off of ourselves and our suffering (the myriad of struggles or heartbreaks we face) and put our focus on the one who suffered and overcame on our behalf. In our pouring out, we are filled afresh with God's unrestrained love.

We worship because it changes us.

In my discouraged and dark moments, I have to make the choice to worship, and not just on Sunday morning. On the other six days of the week, I crank up the music in the kitchen, open my arms wide, and sing, "Here I am to worship, here I am to bow down, here I am to say that you're my God." The kids look at me like I've gone mad, but one day, I pray, they too will feel the need I feel to worship.

Though our children may not fully appreciate the way that worship molds us, let us not underestimate their ability to experience Jesus in worship. And let us model for them a craving for Jesus. We can plant seeds of worship in their hearts and wait in expectation for the way the Spirit of God will carry the grace and truth of God deep into their hearts. For Jesus himself invited children to come near him: "Let the little children come to me, and do not hinder them, for the kingdom of heaven belongs to such as these" (Matt. 19:14).

Actively Pursue Christian Community

Another way to nurture your child's faith is to pursue Christian community by spending time with other families of faith in your free time or through small groups. One of the many benefits of this is that it normalizes the faith experience for our children. Christian community is so important, because the harsh reality is this world is doing its very best to pull our children away from their faith. It teaches them that everything is not only permissible but also beneficial, and it feeds them destructive lies about the way life works best and where happiness can be found. But when we engage in Christian community and give our children the gift of Christian mentors, we teach our children that there are other families who choose, like us, to be *in* the world but not *of* the world. We teach them that real life, abundant life, can be found only in a living, breathing relationship with Christ.

Following Christ is not an uncomplicated or easy thing to do, especially as our children grow into their middle school and high school years. So while Mom and Dad are central and essential to the development of their children's faith, a community of fellow believers can also be incredibly beneficial in helping our kids resist the temptation to listen to the very loud voices of this world that offer our kids endless empty promises.

God has called us to be a part of a body—a hand by itself is useless, but connected to a body it has great power and usefulness (1 Cor. 12:12–30).

Which leads us right to the last seed of faith that nurtures our children's friendship with Jesus—service.

chapter 9

service

*Follow God's example, therefore, as dearly
loved children and walk in the way of love,
just as Christ loved us and gave himself up
for us as a fragrant offering and sacrifice
to God.*

—Ephesians 5:1–2

After reading an inspiring blog by Ann Voskamp about how her family celebrates Christmas, I gathered my boys together and excitedly described my new plan. "This year for Christmas I thought we might try something different! You know how Mommy and Daddy feel about the importance of keeping our hearts centered on the true meaning of Christmas—the gift God gave us in the birth of Jesus Christ. Well, I want our actions to reflect our beliefs, and I don't think we've done a very good job of that so far. While baking a birthday cake for Jesus is fun, and I'm sure he delights in the happy birthday song we sing to him on Christmas Eve, I want our family to experience more, so much more, of the true meaning of Christmas. And one of the ways I thought we might experience more of Christ at Christmas this year is by thinking about what we can give to others instead of focusing on all of the presents we want to get. Perhaps we could serve families who are less fortunate by providing food and gifts to them instead of giving gifts to each other. Wouldn't that be an awesome way to celebrate the gift of Jesus?"

The boys looked at each other, then they looked strangely at me. They sat in silence as they pondered the magnitude of this new plan.

Then Brennan spoke first, simply but profoundly revealing the nature of our human hearts. "Um, Mom, how about we do both? We can give presents, but we can still get presents. Mom, we *need* presents. It's Christmas!"

Cal and Owen nodded in agreement. The plan seemed fair enough to them, as they both chimed in, "Yeah, let's do both!"

"I will give as long as I get." Is this not how the world teaches us to think?

But as Christians, we are called to sacrificial love. To be servants (Mark 9:35), looking not only to our own interests but also to the interests of others (Phil. 2:3–4). We are called to works of service in order to build up the church (Eph. 4:12). As Peter wrote, "Each of you should use whatever gift you have received to serve others, as faithful stewards of God's grace in its various forms" (1 Peter 4:10). And our sacrificial love for others flows from a heart that first remembers Christ's sacrificial love for us.

Inspiring Hearts of Service

So how do we teach our kids about the unexpected blessing that comes from living a life of unlimited generosity, humbly putting others before ourselves through acts of service? How do we teach our kids that because everything we need we already have in Christ Jesus, we are free to give generously of ourselves?

Well, first we must understand what makes us free: the whole-hearted and "limitless" love of Christ.

The late Brennan Manning writes in *The Furious Longing of God*, "The Christian becomes aware that God's appeal for unlimited generosity from His people has been preceded from His side by a limitless love, a love so intent upon a response that He has empowered us to respond through the gift of His own Spirit."[14]

Let me pause here and ask you a hard question. Do you get more focused on teaching your kids about serving others and living generous lives than you do on teaching them how much Jesus loves and accepts them even when they forget or fail to live that way? I do. And it's exhausting because that's not the gospel. I so easily forget that it's only in the wholehearted love of Christ that our hearts are moved from me, me, me to you, you, you.

See, the gospel is the only thing that makes us sincerely pray, "Lord, less of me, more of you." It's in understanding that, by grace, we are free from earning God's love and acceptance through our good works that we are prone to sacrificial love.

So in teaching our children about living lives of sacrificial love, we must start with the gospel—what Jesus has already done for us through his ultimate sacrifice on the cross. Then we pray for God to empower us to live against our selfish nature and in accordance with the nature of Christ, to live in grateful obedience to what the Lord requires of us: "to act justly and to love mercy and to walk humbly with your God" (Mic. 6:8). We pray for hearts that are broken by the same things that break the heart of God, and for bold and selfless faith.

> The gospel is the only thing that makes us sincerely pray, "Lord, less of me, more of you."

And finally, we live out our faith as the hands and feet of Christ in this broken world. No doubt, it's in the "living out" that our hearts are transformed. We will encounter Jesus right in the middle of our acts of service and pursuit of justice. We will find a joy that doesn't crumple as easily as the wrapping paper from the gifts we've opened. And in due time, if not immediately, so will our children. When we plant seeds of service in our children's hearts, we allow them to experience the joy that's hidden in sacrificial love, which we can pray will lead their hearts to a more sustainable pursuit of justice down the road.

Let me share a short story with you to demonstrate our children's ability to desire to serve (*desire* being the key word). A few weeks ago at church, our pastor called the Valentine family onto the stage so the congregation could pray over them before they moved to Uganda as missionaries with the organization Jenga. The Valentines have already raised one amazing son, Ben, who is on staff at our church as a youth pastor. Now they are moving to Uganda with their two younger sons, Will (nine) and Banks (seven). When our pastor asked Will how he felt about leaving the luxuries of home and picking up everything to move to Uganda to serve the poor, he smiled and said, "I'm excited. I've always wanted to be a missionary!"

> To raise children who desire to serve, I need to lead them in *experiencing* sacrificial love.

What? People, my boys are amazing, but I'm wholly confident that Will's answer would not have been their answer. What made this nine-year-old boy desire to serve the poor and be a missionary at such a young age? His family has lived out their faith from the day he was born. They are the living and breathing love of Christ. Now, I'm not saying we all have to drop everything and go be missionaries in a foreign land to raise children who desire to serve. What I am saying is that

Will convicted my mama heart. He taught me, in that one small moment, that to raise children who desire to serve, I need to lead them in *experiencing* sacrificial love.

So now let's look at some of the ways we can help our children experience sacrificial love and plant seeds of service that will reap a harvest of God's love in this world.

Service Begins at Home

Teaching our children about serving one another is a lesson that begins in our own homes. Daily we can point out little opportunities for our kids to serve each other. Perhaps Cal could help Brennan buckle his seat belt or tie his shoe, and Brennan could help Cal put his Legos away or help him find the toy he lost. There are more than enough ways they could share with and serve their baby brother, Owen. No matter what the activity, the point is that they spend plenty of time trying to outdo each other, compete with each other, and prove themselves better than the other, so I remind them to also think about how they can look to the interests of others and serve one another.

When our children struggle with serving one another, we point them to Acts 20:35 (NLV): "We must remember what the Lord Jesus said, 'We are more happy when we give than when we receive.'" We will talk more about this truth in the chapter on cultivating thankfulness in our kids, but for now let me say this: When we ask our kids this one simple question, "Are we more happy when we give or when we receive?" we are not trying to induce guilt, because guilt never changes the heart, but to challenge them to think about the motive of their heart and why their self-interest is prevailing in a particular situation. Then we can lead them in learning to do acts of "Christ-ness."

Random Acts of "Christ-ness"

A dear friend of mine, Courtney Defeo, has inspired thousands of young kids to serve through what she calls "The Light 'Em Up Project."[15] Just a few of her creative ideas include delivering "bags of blessings" to patients on the cardiac floor at the local hospital, handing out ice cold water bottles to exhausted and unappreciated construction workers, delivering sandwiches to the homeless, and loving on the elderly in a nursing home. The possibilities are endless, and the results are priceless.

> Kids are fully capable of experiencing the unexpected blessing that comes from being God's light in this world.

Her example has shown me that kids are fully capable of experiencing the unexpected blessing that comes from being God's light in this world. Even small children can experience the joy that flows from acts of selfless service and encouragement to a world in need of a fresh dose of God's love. We are never too young to grow in our friendship with Jesus by being his hands and feet in this world.

One of the things I love about my husband, Mike, is that he has a huge heart for others, particularly the poor and oppressed. He inspires me in the way he truly lives his life from a place of gratitude and thankfulness for all he has received, and in turn, he is generous with his time, talent, and treasure. I can only pray that this kind of compassion and generosity is something our children will inherit from their father.

Our church has a vibrant mercy ministry, and of course, Mike was drawn to this wonderful group of folks who are focused on transforming our world through the love of God both locally and globally. If he didn't have to work, I am pretty sure this is what he would spend the majority of his time doing. (Well, that and golf.) And because his time with our little ones is precious, Mike tries to participate in projects in which the whole family can participate.

So while our children may not fully understand why we do things such as serve food at a soup kitchen, paint the walls at a women's shelter, help host a holiday BBQ at a homeless shelter, stock the shelves at a food pantry, hand out coats at a coat drive for underprivileged families, or sponsor two beautiful orphans in Rwanda through World Vision, their eyes are being opened to the importance of being God's love and light in this broken world. They are learning about giving generously and valuing others above themselves. And in turn, they are beginning to experience, in small but wonderful ways, the joy and thankfulness that flows from living their lives as an offering to God. Or as my good friend Maureen says, they are learning the joy that comes from "random acts of Christ-ness!"

"Lord, we will do anything, love anyone, and go anywhere. Take our lives and let them be all for thee."

That being said, I want you to know how painfully aware I am of the conviction that God is stirring in my heart for our family in this area. I know he has so much more for us to understand about sacrificial love and service. And this conviction has led me to start praying the prayer, "Lord, we will do anything, love anyone, and go anywhere. Take our lives and let them be all for thee." I'm excited to see how God will answer.

Identify Spiritual Gifts

Jesus said, "By this everyone will know that you are my disciples, if you love one another" (John 13:35). We don't love and serve to make God proud of us, or to earn his love and approval. We serve out of gratitude for how he first served us, by and through his grace. And we serve because "we are God's handiwork, created in Christ Jesus to do good works, which God prepared in advance for us to do" (Eph. 2:10). We can teach our children that our service is an expression of God's unrestrained grace, and an outpouring of who we are in Christ.

As we serve with our children, we receive the privilege of helping them understand and identify their spiritual gifts (1 Cor. 12). One child may uncover a gift of teaching, while another might find a gift of service. You could also explore with them how their talents and interests can be used to serve, both in the church and in the world. Do you have a child who is good at getting other kids to follow him? Show him how to harness that power of leadership in service to others. Do you have a child who loves to sing? Involve her in a music ministry in the church or community. As Paul reminds us, "There are different kinds of gifts, but the same Spirit distributes them. There are different kinds of service, but the same Lord. There are different kinds of working, but in all of them and in everyone it is the same God at work. Now to each one the manifestation of the Spirit is given for the common good" (1 Cor. 12:4–7).

Our gifts are meant to be shared, and in sharing our gifts, we reflect God's infinitely generous heart and magnify the goodness of the Giver. The apostle Paul paints a beautiful picture of just how generous our God is when he writes, in Romans 8:31–32, "If God is for us, who can be against us? He who did not spare his own Son, but gave him up for us all—how will he not also, along with him, graciously give us all things?"

We grow in our friendship with Jesus as we live as his light in this dark world. As we carry his torch of hope into a seemingly hopeless circumstance, we experience his love more intimately for us and for the one we serve. We are all precious in his sight, and serving one another connects us under the banner of "No, not one is righteous"

(Rom. 3:10–12). It reminds us, as the great hymn proclaims, that our "hope is built on nothing less than Jesus' blood and righteousness."

Summary

My hope is that throughout this section, you have seen how important it is that we as parents stay "attached to the vine" and nurture our own relationships with Jesus as we set out to lead our children in their own vibrant friendship with him. We must allow Jesus to do his good work within us so that we can pour out his love into our kids. Prayer, Bible reading, Scripture memorization, worship, and service are not just "something else we must do." Rather, they are gifts God uses to open our hearts for what he wants to do for us, in us, and through us! Through the life-giving seeds of faith we have explored here, we can nurture our children's trust in and friendship with Jesus. And as you will see in the following section, Christlike character—the fruit of his Spirit that we, as parents, so desire to see in our kids' lives—is the overflow of a friendship with Jesus. Yes, the friendship precedes the fruit!

part 3

···

growing in Christlike character

chapter 10

the fruit of grace

He gives us everything we need for life and
for holy living. He gives it through His great
power. As we come to know Him better, we
learn that He called us to share His own
shining-greatness and perfect life.

—2 Peter 1:3 NLV

"House Rules." This expression is where our family's journey into freedom began. While my parenting was still mired in perfection and performance, I identified a long list of house rules, put them on the fridge, and essentially said, "Kids, these are our family rules, and you will obey them." It's like pretending that a clearly posted 55 mph speed limit sign makes me want to go 55 mph. When the truth is it actually makes me want to go 62 mph—just fast enough that I can get to my destination sooner but not get punished for disobeying the law.

See, without realizing it, I sadly believed that more clearly posting our rules was going to help our boys more perfectly live a life of obedience. I was employing pure behavior modification, and we were a fast moving train-wreck!

Over time, I began to realize we can't *make* our kids grow in Christlike character any more than we can make ourselves grow in Christlike character. Grace alone is what "teaches us to say 'No' to ungodliness and worldly passions, and to live self-controlled, upright and godly lives in this present age" (Titus 2:12).

Seriously, think about the last time you decided to *make* yourself more kind, or more thankful, or Lord help us, more patient. How long did your efforts last? How much joy did you experience? This stuff has to be the fruit of his Spirit at work in our lives, not the result of guilt, force, or fear. We are powerless to make our kids desire to love what he loves and do what he'd do. In fact, we are best served by actually embracing our inability to change our kids and accepting that only his radical grace, stirred in their hearts by the power of the Holy Spirit, inspires devotion and a desire to live in his likeness.

Am I saying we shouldn't give our kids rules? Of course not. We must teach our children God's law and his command for obedience to him and to us. What I am saying is that we trust entirely too much in our own finite resources and entirely too little in God's infinite grace to mold us, and our children, into his image.

> We trust entirely too much in our own finite resources and entirely too little in God's infinite grace to mold us, and our children, into his image.

Yes, this list of house rules is where God began the transformation in our family, from a focus on God's rules (which we will also refer to as God's law) to a focus on God's grace. Instead of thinking I can manufacture virtue in my boys, I am learning to turn that work over to God, to be a "truth bearer" not a "fruit counter" in my children's lives. I am learning that Christlike virtues are the fruit of grace. So let's explore what this good news means for our parenting.

Why Does Jesus Give Us Rules?

You and I both know the very word *rules* has many negative connotations. It would be easy for a child (and an adult, for that matter) to equate the word *rules* (or *commandments* or *laws*) with a long list of controlling, suffocating "shall and shall-nots" for rigid obedience. Therefore, before we proceed with talking about how we can use the commandments of Christ to help our children grow in Christlike character, we must first answer the pivotal question, "Well, why *does* Jesus give us rules?" and then explore how we can translate this important knowledge to our children.

So ask yourself, "Why does Jesus call us to be peacemakers? Why does he instruct us to give thanks in all circumstances? Why does he teach us to treat others the way that we want to be treated?"

Is it because Jesus is a religious zealot, profoundly serious and solemn? Does he delight in us only when we obey, and shame us when we don't? Is his love for us predicated on our obedience and good works? Does he give us commandments to control us, to suck the life out of us? Is he a kill-joy with a big stick in one hand trying to keep us in line and a checklist in his other hand keeping track of whether we are doing more good than bad?

Or is it because Jesus is *for* us; because he loves us with a ravenous, constantly pursuing, lavish, and extravagant love? Is his delight over us because of who we are as his beloved children, created in his image and redeemed by his blood? Are his instructions for righteous living an invitation to experience a more intimate relationship with him? Are his commandments intended to equip and bless us for the purpose for which we were each so wonderfully created, to glorify him in thought, word, and deed? Is his call to obedience actually the blueprint to abundant life and freedom from slavery to sin?

You see, the Jesus whom we find consistently and unequivocally woven throughout Scripture fits the latter of these two descriptions. And this is the wondrous knowledge that we must impart to our kids when we teach them about growing in Christlike character.

Jesus said, "The thief comes only to steal and kill and destroy; I have come that they may have life, and have it to the full" (John 10:10). Jesus is describing the kind of life he came to give us: a life of freedom, life to the fullest, abundant life. While the "thief" comes to steal our joy, kill our peace, and destroy our fullness of life, Jesus' desire for us, and for our children, is freedom and the fullness of joy. Not the kind of joy that the world offers but the kind that can be found only in an intimate relationship with him.

Now, we certainly don't want to suggest to our kids that a life lived in obedience to Christ will result in pure joyful abundance. Scripture is very clear that just as Jesus Christ suffered, so too will we. The Christian remains vulnerable to trials, temptations, and heartaches of every kind. What we can teach our kids is that our suffering need not separate us from Christ. Rather, our suffering allows us to identify with Christ, who endured the ultimate suffering by choosing separation from his Father to atone for the sin of the world on the cross (2 Cor. 5:21).

His heart broke so that ours could heal. As we read in Isaiah 53:3, "He was despised and rejected by mankind, a man of suffering, and familiar with pain." So when our souls ache, we can know with confidence that Christ not only thoroughly knows the depths of our pain but also can be trusted with our sorrow. He is fully present in our time of need, and he carries us in his strong, competent arms when we cannot take the next step. He is, as we read in Psalm 34:18, "close to the brokenhearted and saves those who are crushed in spirit." Yes, even in our pain, we can remain in his abundant love, we can have his peace that passes all understanding, and we can have faith that our joy will return to us, whether in this life or in the life to come. We know he is working all things together for our good and for his glory (Rom. 8:28).

Now, if you are wondering how this has anything to do with parenting a wholehearted child, I don't blame you! But please stay with me here because I'm confident of this: If our desire is to see our kids grow in Christlike character, we must start by captivating them with his grace. Our kids must *know* something about Jesus' heart for them before they will ever *desire* to seek his heart above all else!

Charles Spurgeon described it best when he wrote, "When I thought God was hard, I found it easy to sin; but when I found God so kind, so good, so overflowing with compassion, I smote upon my breast to think that I could ever have rebelled against One who loved me so, and sought my good."

The Overflow of the Heart

The radical grace of Jesus wells up in us the desire to love him and our neighbor, and the inexhaustible power of the Holy Spirit empowers us to love him and our neighbor. "Christlike character" is the overflow of a heart that has been captivated by his grace and empowered by the Holy Spirit! This is the message we need to be translating to our kids.

The gospel of Luke points us to this idea of heart overflow. He writes, "A good person produces good things from the treasury of a good heart, and an evil person produces evil things from the treasury of an evil heart. What you say flows from what is in your heart" (Luke 6:45 NLT). And in Proverbs 4:23 we find this wise instruction regarding the heart: "Above all else, guard your heart, for everything you do flows from it."

Now, perhaps you have heard a lot of talk about the importance of "focusing on your child's heart" during times of training and disciplining. I certainly have. It's a hot topic, and for good reason — it's true. So let's start by clarifying what that expression means.

● ● ● ● ● ● ● ● ● ● ● ● ● ● ● ● ●

"Christlike character" is the overflow of a heart that has been captivated by his grace and empowered by the Holy Spirit!

● ● ● ● ● ● ● ● ● ● ● ● ● ● ● ●

When we say "focus on your child's heart," we are saying "belief motivates behavior." Plain and simple. We need to get to the belief behind the behavior, because our beliefs dictate our attitudes and actions. The real issue is a belief issue, not a behavioral issue.

God cares about the heart behind the obedience, and Jesus demonstrated this time and time again. Whenever he spoke, he went right to the heart. He saw past the performance and pretending of the religious rule-followers and addressed what was going on beneath their outside behavior. In fact, Jesus reserved his harshest criticism for those who did everything right on the outside but were "far from him" in their hearts.

Just like Jesus, we need to go right to the hearts of our children, helping them to see the sinful belief (nature) that leads to their sinful behavior, as I will show in chapter 20, "Discipline and Correction." The heart behind that behavior is usually a heart that wants what it wants when it wants it. A heart in rebellion to God.

Now that we've established what it means to "focus on your child's heart," the next question we need to answer is, *How* should a parent focus on the heart? Should we merely point out how our child's bad behavior is showing their sinful heart? And is it safe to assume that if we show them their sinful nature, they will be motivated to change and do the right thing?

No! A thousand times, no.

Behavior modification does nothing to change the heart, nor

does merely asking our children the right questions to reveal their sinful hearts. We are just as mistaken to assume we can harness the heart as we are to assume we can create virtues in our children through behavior modification. Our role is to teach them how to live godly lives, help them understand their sin and their need for Jesus, and to surrender them to the Holy Spirit, who convicts us and makes us hungry for his grace. To do otherwise is to play God in our children's lives. And I don't know about you, but I want *God* to be their God, not me.

Which leads me to a scary conclusion. Some children who are shown Jesus' grace will take advantage of it or even reject it. Does that make me a failure as a parent? No. Does that invalidate grace? Absolutely not. The fact that our children will take advantage of grace does not negate the power and the purpose of grace. And it certainly doesn't mean we should stop giving and showing grace when we don't see its fruit right away. The fruit of grace is almost always in the future. Our job as parents is to facilitate the work of the Spirit rather than frustrate it (Eph. 6:4). To plant seeds of his unconditional love in our children's hearts and entrust them to his care, knowing that the fruit of grace (Christlikeness) is never dependent on my heart questions and work as a parent but rather on the Holy Spirit's transforming power.

A Family Verse and Six Virtues

By now you may be thinking, "All this theology is well and good, but how do I translate this thinking into my parenting?" So now let's talk specifics! Our family's process (which may differ from yours) went something like this. Mike and I began by thinking about who our children are, and who we wanted to help them become—not in the professional golfer, famous country singer, or Supreme Court justice kind of way—but the kind of heart we hoped they would have for Jesus and the kind of light we prayed they would be in this world.

The next step was to involve Cal and Brennan in the process. (We assumed full power of attorney for Owen, who was just a newborn at the time.) We wanted our kids to have a sense of ownership in the process, and we wanted them to know their input was valuable, so we asked them to share with us what they thought the Bible teaches us about Jesus and what they felt was important in our family.

> The fact that our children will take advantage of grace does not negate the power and the purpose of grace.

Following our conversation with the kids, Mike and I identified a family verse: "'Love the Lord your God with all your heart and with all your soul and with all your mind.' This is the first and greatest commandment. And the second is like it: 'Love your neighbor as yourself'" (Matt. 22:37–39).

We chose this verse not only because it's the first and greatest commandment but also because it reminds us that love is the source from which the virtues will flow.

We then identified six virtues we wanted to focus on to help our kids grow in Christlike character. Those six virtues are:

- Respect
- Self-control
- Kindness
- Thankfulness
- Peacemaking
- Honesty

These six virtues are not listed in any particular order, and they don't include *all* of the things we hope to teach our children. They do, however, reflect the ways in which we hope to teach our children to love what Jesus loves and to do what Jesus would do. We also chose several Bible verses to use as the foundation to each of the virtues, as you will see in each of the chapters where we explain the virtues.

The next step was to decide what to call these virtues. We chose The Fruit of Grace as an important daily reminder that when we teach our kids what is good and right and true, we aren't giving them a checklist of the ways they must "do more, be better, and try harder" to be more like Christ. Holiness isn't a destination but rather is the person of Jesus, who makes his home inside our hearts and transforms us into his image through the power of his Spirit. The virtues are the overflow, the fruit of his grace.

> Holiness isn't a destination but rather is the person of Jesus, who makes his home inside our hearts and transforms us into his image through the power of his Spirit.

The final step was to create a poster that listed our virtues and the verses that accompany them. We took out our markers, stickers, scissors, and glue, and together we drew a house and filled it in with our list. None of us is particularly artistic, especially me, so let me assure you the house we drew was uninspiring, at best. Nonetheless, we did it together, and we were proud.

On the roof we wrote all of our names, including our dog, Henry (Brennan's idea). At the very top of the roof we put a cross as a reminder of who is ultimately the head of our family. I would take a picture of the final product and present it to you if I could. Unfortunately, Owen tore the masterpiece off the fridge and ate a good portion of it. It's probably best left to the imagination anyway.

The Fine Print

And finally, the fine print—the last, but crucial, piece before we dig into each of the virtues.

Now, we all know what *fine print* is, that information written in very small print at the bottom of the page that we don't want to read but we know is important. Well, the fine print of teaching our kids to grow in his likeness is simply this: avoid double standards. This was a very hearty lesson for Mike and me.

You see, if we teach our children about Christlike character, but we choose not to model what a life in Christ looks like, we teach in vain. We must rely on the power of the Holy Spirit to help us teach *and* model these virtues to our children. Therefore, as we explore the six virtues in the following chapters, I will intertwine how we as parents can model a life in Christ and how it can be taught to our children.

Now before it sounds like the responsibility of reaching (and transforming) your child's heart all depends on you, let me offer you a straight shot of hope.

Yes, as parents we must somehow demonstrate (in small, imperfect, and fallible ways) the love Jesus has demonstrated to us and what the response to this grace looks like. But I can assure you I fall short each and every day in modeling these traits to our kids. And herein lies the hope! While it is important that I model Christlike character for our kids, it's significantly more important that I model for them what God's grace looks like in my life. Just as our kids will understand kindness or respect or thankfulness as it is modeled for them, so too will they understand grace if we model our own need for it. See, I used to think that my primary role as a parent was to model Christlike character for our kids, and when I failed, I would beat myself up. But the more I grow in my understanding of grace and the unconditional love of Christ for me, the more I realize that while Christlike living is important, it is significantly more important that I be authentic about my trust in and need for Jesus.

I must be willing to tell my kids, "Me too! I struggle with sin too. I am not perfect either, and I need forgiveness as much as you. Thank God for Jesus, who already paid the price for our sin and covers us with his perfect righteousness. Even on our worst days, God is not mad at me, and God is not mad at you. He smiles on us and is pleased with us as his beloved children because of our trust and faith in what Jesus Christ did for us."

We can use our sin and failure to teach our kids that being a lover and a follower of Christ

> While it is important that I model Christlike character for our kids, it's significantly more important that I model for them what God's grace looks like in my life.

doesn't mean we are going to get it right all of the time. It only means that we have put our trust in the only one who did, and we are therefore forgiven and unconditionally loved when we don't get it right. Of course this doesn't mean that we go on sinning so that his grace can abound (Rom. 6:1). It just means that we are free to confess that we are imperfect people loved by a perfect God.

Authenticity allows grace to reign. You don't have to be perfect or parent perfectly for your kids to grow in Christlike character. You only need to know that his grace is sufficient and his power is made perfect in your weakness (2 Cor. 12:9). Yes, *his* power is made perfect in *your* weakness. He can use even your weaknesses and mistakes as a parent for his glory.

There is so. much. freedom. in embracing the fact that our primary purpose is not to point to ourselves as the ultimate model for our children but to point away from ourselves and to Jesus. He is the only one who has never, and will never, let them down. He is their perfection, not us! Or as Hebrews 12:2 puts it, "Let us keep looking to Jesus. Our faith comes from Him and He is the One Who makes it perfect" (NLV).

In the rest of this section, I offer ideas to teach and equip your *young* children to grow in Christlike character through the six virtues of respect, self-control, kindness, thankfulness, peacemaking, and honesty. But let's not forget, though our job is to teach our children how to grow in God's image and love, to equip them with skills for godly living, and to help them understand their sin when their hearts are in rebellion, we must keep this important question in the forefront of our minds as we go about our parenting: "Am I solely focused on what I want my kids to be doing to be more like Jesus, or am I pointing my kids back to their need for Jesus and what he has already done for them?"

And on that note, let's dive into the first virtue, respect, and explore how we can create a climate of grace in which respect and all the other virtues can thrive!

> Authenticity allows grace to reign.

chapter 11

respect

*Exercise your freedom by serving God, not by
breaking the rules. Treat everyone you meet
with dignity. Love your spiritual family.
Revere God. Respect the government.*
—1 Peter 2:16–17 MSG

One day when we were enjoying a beautiful day at the neighborhood pool, Brennan came running over and informed me that an older boy was picking on him. "Mom," he loudly declared, "that boy isn't being nice. He's pushing me in the water and telling me I can't play in the pool!"

"I'm so sorry, baby. I know that must have hurt your feelings. What did you say to him when he pushed you?"

Brennan declared, "I told him to go pick on somebody his own size! Was that the right thing to say, Mommy?"

Don't ask me where he learned that expression. I can only assume it was his version of "treat others the way you want to be treated" (a verse we emphasize with our children) because *everyone* wants to be treated with respect.

"Treat others the way that you want to be treated" comes from Matthew 7:12, and it seems to reach down deep with little ones. For example, if Cal is including Owen in something but he is leaving Brennan out, I may ask him, "Are you treating Brennan the way you want to be treated? How does it make you feel when someone at school leaves you out of a game?" Or if Brennan yanks a toy out of Owen's hand, I may ask him, "Are you treating Owen the way you like to be treated? Do you like it when someone bigger and stronger takes things from you without asking?" In my asking these questions, the boys are learning to think about how their actions affect others and how to treat them with respect.

Asking questions is key. (And you'll continue to find that asking questions rather than offering statements is a theme in this book.) When possible, I encourage you to ask questions rather than offer statements, as questions are so much more effective than statements when we are trying to reach our children's hearts. For instance, if we simply tell them to treat others the way they want to be treated, our statement is likely to go in one ear and out the other. However, if we ask a question, our kids are required to think deeply about what they are doing and how it affects others, which can teach empathy, compassion, and of course, respect.

• • • • • • • • • • • • • • • • •

Asking questions is key.

• • • • • • • • • • • • • • • • •

I also have to ask myself, "Are you treating the kids the way you would want to be treated?" We tend to think that children should respect their parents, but do we believe our children also deserve to be treated and spoken to with respect? Respect is not just *the state of being regarded with honor or esteem* but also *a willingness to show appreciation and consideration*. As we model consideration for our children, they will learn to return that consideration to us. This is full-circle respect.

Fearing the Lord

Teaching our children about respect begins with teaching them what it means to fear the Lord. We see this expression over and over again throughout Scripture, and it can be so easily misunderstood. See, fearing the Lord does not mean that we should want to run and hide from God, that he is out to get us and punish us for our wrongdoing. No, the Lord is not the "roaring lion seeking whom he can devour" (1 Peter 5:8). Fearing the Lord means to stand in awe and wonder of God. To bask in his power, his sufficiency, his sovereignty, his greatness, and oh yes, his unfathomable grace. The fear of the Lord is rooted in his love, in our awareness of his perfection and holiness, and in our desire to be in unity with him. It's holy fear.

As we stand in awe and wonder of his sovereignty *and* his grace, our hearts are stirred to trust and obey. Our hearts are stirred to exercise our freedom in Christ to serve God rather than to abuse our freedom as a pass to do as we please (Ps. 103:11–18). And because every human being bears the image of God, we can teach our children that showing love and respect to humankind without distinction is another way we can serve God and honor one another.

Respect for Authority

A key element of respect is teaching our children the importance of honoring adults and submitting to those in authority. First Peter 5:5 teaches this truth: "You who are younger, submit yourselves to your elders." Our children understand our expectation that they treat everyone—their teachers, their friend's parents, and the fast-food clerk—with respect. But just because they know this is what we expect doesn't mean it always happens.

For example, our children know that when we introduce them to an adult, they are expected to look into the adult's eyes, and speak a clear and friendly, "Hello, Mr. Jones." But if Cal, for instance, turns his head and pretends to be shy when an adult says, "Hi, Cal, nice to meet you," I will quietly ask him, "Cal, are you showing respect to Mr. Jones? Please greet Mr. Jones like the gentleman you are." It's a lot less about manners and a lot more about treating people, particularly those in authority, with respect. Therefore, if you have a particularly shy child, you may want to kneel down beside them, put your arm around them, and stay firm in your expectation that shyness is not an excuse for showing disrespect.

As the parents of three boys, we are keenly aware of the need to teach the boys not only what it means to be respectful of adults but also what the Bible teaches us about how men should honor and be respectful of women. Our boys will indeed learn from Mike's example what it means to treat women with respect. Even at a very young age they are watching and learning how to show respect in little ways, with our great hope being this will set the stage for show-ing respect in bigger ways later on.

Modeling Respect

As parents, one of the ways we model treating one another with dig-nity and respect is through our communication with one another. For instance, if Daddy bosses Mommy around, our children wonder why they can't be bossy with Mommy. And if Mommy is disre-spectful to Daddy, our children wonder why Daddy is deserving of their respect. Even in an argument, we can teach our children about respectful communication by avoiding insults and resolving the argument with affection. Or apologizing when we don't!

Yes, our children learn about treating one another with respect by watching how we speak to one another, but it's equally important to note that our children learn about respect by observing the way we listen to each other.

Listening in Action

When I called Mike at work to discuss our evening plans, I identified the sound of computer keys tapping in the background on his end of the call. Recognizing that he was working rather than listening, I began talking nonsense. I said something about how the shoe in the road that fell off a tree was yellow and red, and was in the way of the horse carriage, and oh, I like licorice. When I was done with my gibberish, I paused briefly and asked, "Is that okay, honey?" And sure enough my husband responded, "Okay, baby, sounds great!"

> When it comes to modeling respectful communication, there is nothing more meaningful we can do than listen.

Now before it sounds like I'm throwing my husband under the bus, I should note that Mike is actually the natural listener in the relationship. Listening is Mike's forte (when he's not at work, at least!). I, on the other hand, have to concentrate on being quick to listen and slow to speak (James 1:19).

When it comes to modeling respectful communication, there is nothing more meaningful we can do than listen. I can't emphasize this enough—we must, must listen. And listening well requires that we learn how to talk *with* our children, rather than at them. If we talk at them, they will come to learn that we do not respect their feelings or their thoughts, and we are merely concerned with being heard, venting our frustration, and seeing them obey. However, if we talk with them, and we are thoughtful about understanding what's in their heart, we send a message that what they feel and what they have to say is worthy of being heard. We affirm their worth when we try to see the world through their eyes.

Take a moment to read the following poem, and imagine your child as the one saying these words to you.

When I ask you to listen to me
and you start giving advice,
you have not done what I asked.
When I ask you to listen to me
and you begin to tell me why I shouldn't feel that way,
you are trampling on my feelings.
When I ask you to listen to me
and you feel you have to do something to solve my
      problem,
you have failed me, strange as that may seem.
Listen! All I asked was that you listen.
Not to talk or do—just hear me.
When you do something for me that I can and need to do
      for myself,
you contribute to my fear and weakness.
But when you accept as a single fact that I do feel what I
      feel, no matter how irrational,
then I can quit trying to convince you
and get to the business of understanding what's behind
      this feeling.
So, please listen and just hear me.
And if you want to talk, wait a minute for your turn;
      and I'll listen to you.

—"Please Listen," author unknown

Listening is one of the ways we model God's heart, because our heavenly Father is indeed quick to listen. He is not a God who says, "I am God and you are not, so I'll do the talking and you'll do the listening." Nobody listens better than God. And modeling thoughtful listening for our kids opens the door to training them how to pay attention and gain understanding (Prov. 4:1–2).

To model thoughtful listening, do the obvious: stop what you are doing. Look up from your screen (whatever screen that may be!). Get down to their level. Make eye contact. Turn your full attention their way. And trust me when I tell you I'm preaching this one to myself. Too often we put off our kids' needs and questions until they are convenient for us to deal with, when sometimes just a few seconds of interaction are needed to resolve an issue or question. That is not to say that our kids should feel free to interrupt at any time; obviously there are limits. But in general, modeling thoughtful listening to our kids sets the stage for us to require it of our kids.

When we model a listening ear to our children, they know that they can say anything to Mommy and Daddy, as long as they do it in a respectful way. We want them to be honest with their feelings and frustrations and needs, but we do require that the words and tone be respectful. And at the end of the day, when the conversation has been had and each party has been heard, they know that even if they don't agree with us, they must still respect us.

Can You Hear My Voice?

One simple but profound way we can train our children to pay attention and listen is by beginning our request with a simple, "Can you hear my voice?"

For example, three rows back in the family minivan, the children cannot hear my voice easily. If I need to get their attention while I am driving, the first question I ask before I say anything of substance is, "Kids, can you hear my voice?"

So often I would get frustrated with our kids for not listening to me or to my instructions, when in fact, much of the problem was that I had not set them up to listen well. Now I know, and they have learned, that if the answer to my question is "Yes, I can hear your voice," they have just committed to listening to what comes next. The accountability begins at "Yes, Mommy, I can hear your voice."

Even when the children are sitting right next to me, they some-times cannot "hear" my voice because they have become so engrossed in a book, a show, or an imaginary game. It isn't until I ask, "Can you hear my voice?" that they know I need their full attention.

Repeat and Complete

Another way we can hone respectful listening in our children is by asking them to repeat what we've asked of them before sending them off to complete a task. Saying, "Please repeat to Mommy what I just asked of you," is also how I know whether they're implementing selective listening or if they actually heard, "It's time to leave for school. I need you to go to the front door and put your shoes on."

Research actually reveals that children are more likely to act on something to which they have verbally committed. So teach your children to verbally respond to your request, *repeat*, and commit to take action, *complete*. For instance, when I ask the boys to complete a task, I have taught them to say "Okay, Mommy" or "Yes, Mommy" in response to what I've asked of them. "Yes, Mommy" or "Okay, Mommy" means "I have listened to you, and now I commit to obey-ing you."

This technique takes practice, but it's well worth the effort. When I first decided to try this at home, I followed up almost every request with "Cal, please say 'Yes, Mommy'" or "Cal, please say 'Okay, Mommy.'" I asked him to verbally commit to obeying. And in time, with a little practice, Cal (and now Brennan and Owen) have learned that "Yes, Mommy" or "Okay, Mommy" is the respect-ful response I expect to hear when I ask them not only to listen but *also* to obey.

Using this method eliminates a lot of frustration and leads to more peaceful communication. Which mom would you want to live with, the one who repeats herself till she goes blue in the face, then blows her stack? Or the mom who makes sure the first time that you have listened, who makes her request respectfully, and who requires a respectful word and action in response? Not only that, but boy, do I get tired of hearing myself talk. Over and over and over again, my voice, ringing in their ears and mine. Teaching our kids how to listen and respond respectfully can eliminate a great deal of this. (And simply remembering that this season of intense and draining training will not last forever doesn't hurt either!)

The Trouble with Pride

When our children struggle with respect, I find it's usually rooted in pride. I was recently reminded of the pride I had as a child when we spent some time with a lovely couple who taught Sunday school when I was young, and they shared a story I had long forgotten (or perhaps just suppressed). Evidently I was a pretty entitled preacher's kid, and on one particular Sunday morning while I was misbehaving in Sunday school, my teacher told me I would be asked to leave the classroom and return to the service with my parents if I did not change my behavior. My response to her (which I can't believe I am about to share with you) was "Do you have any idea who I am?" Oh yes, I had my fair share of pride.

Pride rears its ugly head when our children inherit a glorified sense of importance or superiority, or when they do not like the fact that they must submit to God and to us. The Bible, and particularly Proverbs, is loud and clear about the destructive results of pride—our pride brings us low; it breeds quarrels; it brings disgrace. Therefore, as parents, we must be thoughtful about helping our children understand the destructive results of pride and take time to help them understand the belief (me, me, me) that motivates pride. When we do find pride creeping into our children's little souls, we must remind them how God calls and equips us to treat one another.

Rudeness and Whining

When our kids struggle to show respect, it tends to come in the form of rudeness or whining. For instance, if a demand, rather than a request, is made for something, I will remind our children that I will not respond to rudeness and that they must speak with respect. When they speak to me, or any adult for that matter, with a command or demand, my response usually sounds something like "Brennan, if you would like me to listen to you, you may ask with respect." Or "Cal, you cannot tell Mommy what to do. If you expect a response, you need to ask me your question again respectfully."

And if I hear something from one of my kids along the lines of "Maaa-uumm," which grates on me like the sound of fingernails on a chalkboard, I know the rest of the sentence will also be some sort of whine festival, and not the kind of wine festival I like to attend. Therefore, when our children whine, my response tends to be "Please find a respectful way to talk to me. I will not respond to anything you say when you are disrespectful."

Note that saying, "I will not respond to anything you say," is different from saying, "I cannot hear anything you say," because the truth is we can indeed hear them; we just refuse to respond when the tone or the words are disrespectful. Why is this important? Well, in time our children will have the skills to think, "Mom's not telling the truth. She *can* hear me but she is saying she can't." The distinction may seem harmless, but we will talk more about the effect of little white lies when we get to the virtue of honesty.

In due time, we will expand the conversation on respect to include the topic of self-respect and the ways in which we are called to honor God with our bodies. Understanding that they were "bought with a price" and that the Spirit of God takes up residence in their bodies will be a crucial conversation down the road (1 Cor. 6:19 – 20). For now, we are setting the stage for respect.

Teaching respect, even in the little things, begins at home in their relationship with us. As one of my great heroes, Billy Graham, has said, "A child who is allowed to be disrespectful to his parents will not have true respect for anyone."

chapter 12
self-control

For the Spirit God gave us does not make
us timid, but gives us power, love
and self-discipline.
—2 Timothy 1:7

In the midst of one of Brennan's three-year-old temper tantrums, I jokingly asked, "Brennan, baby, why are you melting?" (Although fun for me, sarcasm is rarely useful in these situations.) Hence, "I am going to melt!" are the words Brennan declares when he knows he's upset and is having trouble with self-control. These are the days when almost right out of the gate, I can tell he's ready for battle, because the smallest thing can trigger a rushing waterfall of emotions. And I know, on this kind of day, I will find myself saying, more often than I want to count, "Brennan, ask Jesus to give you a spirit of self-control."

In 2 Timothy 1:7 we are reminded that the Spirit God gives us is one of "power, love and self-discipline." The key word is *gives*. He gives, and we take hold. When we take hold of the spirit of self-discipline, or self-control, we restrain ourselves from saying or doing something that may make us feel better in the short term but isn't for our, or anyone else's, good in the long term.

At this chaotic stage in our lives, I have to daily remind myself to take hold of this spirit of self-control. When the kids are wreaking havoc and I'm ready to lose it, I have to remember that when I lose my self-control and I don't treat our children with respect, I essentially teach them to do the same. But if I recognize that they are watching me and learning from me, and I take hold of a spirit of power and self-control, then I have the ability to bear with our children in love, gentleness, and patience (Eph. 4:1 – 3).

Patience

In the wise words of Charles Spurgeon, "Patience is a grace as difficult as it is necessary, and as hard to come by as it is precious when it is gained." Patience, such a precious and rare commodity. I know few moms who don't struggle with it, and my children know all too well about my personal struggle with patience.

For example, recently when I picked Brennan up from school, I gave him the same big smile and huge hug I always give him when he runs into my arms at pickup.

When he left my embrace he asked, "Mom, where's Cal?"

I offered my best sales pitch. "Cal has a play date today, buddy. But you get to hang with Owen and me!"

Evidently that was not the kind of day Brennan had in mind. In the blink of an eye he ripped off his backpack and threw it across the schoolyard, fell to the ground, and yelled, "That's so not fair, Mom!" My son, who typically radiates joy, was "melting" before my very eyes.

With lots of curious moms looking my way, I knelt down in front of Brennan and before I said a word to him, I prayed aloud, "Lord, this is an emergency! I need your heart and I need it now. Please give me—"

But before I could get another word out, Brennan finished my sentence. "Patience. Mommy needs patience." Yes, my children know my weaknesses well. Mommy needs help with patience.

Patience, in the dictionary, is defined as:

1. Quiet steady perseverance
2. Even-tempered care
3. Bearing of difficult circumstance, of being provoked, of being annoyed, and of being delayed *without* anger, complaining, or losing your temper

When I read this definition of patience, my mind immediately wanders to how Jesus relates to me. My senseless worry and self-inflicted angst could easily make him declare, "Oh, Jeannie, you are so exhausting!" but instead, he is patient. He is so very patient. When there is a lesson I refuse to learn, where there is a blessing I feel unworthy to accept, when there is a doubt I cling to for dear life, when there is a worry I milk for all it's worth, he is so very patient with me.

And out of this knowledge, I often pray aloud in front of our children when I am on the verge of losing my cool: "O Lord, how I long to be the patient parent you are to me. Protect me from the inclination to lose my self-control. I desperately need an infusion of your patience. Give me a new heart that desires to glorify you, and help me model your gentle and patient heart to my kids."

> "O Lord, how I long to be the patient parent you are to me."

You see, in Cal's earlier years I had simplified the definition of patience to merely "waiting for what you want." If he would interrupt me or continue to ask me for something after I had instructed him to "please wait," I would say, "Cal, you must have patience — please tell Mommy what patience is." And Cal would respond, "Patience is waiting for what you want." While I think my old definition of patience was a good place to start, it certainly wasn't a good place to end. Now I know I also needed to teach the children about patience as "quiet steady perseverance and bearing of difficult circumstances without losing your self-control."

React or Respond?

Teaching our children about patience in this way required my taking an honest look at the ways in which I was contributing to the havoc. You see, in the midst of the chaos of our daily lives, I have two choices. I can react or I can respond. Losing my self-control and raising my voice would be a reaction, whereas choosing self-control and maintaining a respectful tone would be a response. It's an important life lesson I want our kids to learn early on, but trust me when I tell you it is *not* one I have mastered. Nonetheless, here is what I am learning. If I react to the chaos, I am caught up in the heat of the moment and I allow my emotions to drive my actions and the outcome. However, if I respond to the chaos, I am choosing to be self-controlled and thoughtful by first carefully weighing how the alternatives will affect the outcome. This approach is the opposite of an impulsive reaction, where responses are made without forethought.

> In the heat of the moment — in the heat of the very real war that is raging for my soul — what I need most is not a plan. I need Jesus.

Now before we go any further in talking about how we can choose a spirit of self-control, I want to pause and say this: in those times of crisis when frustration, anger, or whatever other emotion is about to make us lose it, what we need most in that moment is Jesus. It's that simple. I need Jesus in me to live through me. I can plan and plot and try to manipulate my emotions all I want. But in the heat of the moment—in the heat of the very real war that is raging for my soul— what I need most is not a plan. I need Jesus. And modeling this for our kids is one of the greatest gifts we can give them. We need Jesus to rescue us from ourselves first and foremost, and yes, we need Jesus to help us respond rather than react. In the wise words of Tim Keller, "Self-control is not willpower, it's gospel power." So let's now look at how this concept is applicable to our children's lives and explore some of the ways in which we can equip them to have a spirit of self-control.

Help Them Understand and Put Words to Their Emotions

In 2 Peter 1:5–7 we learn about a few of the virtues that are part of a fruitful Christian life: "For this very reason, make every effort to add to your faith goodness; and to goodness, knowledge; and to knowledge, self-control; and to self-control, perseverance; and to perseverance, godliness; and to godliness, mutual affection; and to mutual affection, love."

I am particularly fond of what we learn about the virtues that come specifically before and after self-control, "and to knowledge, self-control; and to self-control, perseverance."

One of the ways we train our children in self-control is through knowledge, by helping them understand and put words to their emotions. Since frustration and anger are often the primary emotions that tempt us, and our children, to lose our self-control, I want to start there.

Now, I've been told more than once that little kids "gotta get it out" (which is why we own a small trampoline and why I just ordered a punching bag!). And I'm all for the "get it out." It's just *how* they get it out that matters. For example, when Brennan was about two and a half years old and Owen was born, Brennan's temper flared. And when it flared he would use his hands (and his feet and his teeth) to show his anger. He would get very physical with whomever or whatever had upset him. Hence began two very helpful expressions we commonly use with our kids to help them choose self-control.

The first is, "Show me your hands." When their hands have started to fly and they no longer see each other as fellow human beings but as personal punching bags, I say, "Stop and show me your hands." After they put their hands out as I've asked, I say, "Show me where your hands belong," and they put their hands on their belly. This exercise is very effective in getting them to stop using their hands on each other and put them back where they belong.

The other expression we use is, "Use your words, not your hands." Once the hands have stopped flying, we teach them to use their words to problem solve. But in order for our kids to use their words, I have to help them identify their emotions. They need to recognize what they were feeling before they entered into a complete downward spiral. You know what I'm talking about when I say "downward spiral." We've all witnessed it, and it isn't pretty. When Brennan is headed down this path, I take both of his hands in mine, look into his eyes, and say, "Brennan, I know you are frustrated, but you must use your words, not your hands." And then I may follow that up with, "Now please tell Mommy what's wrong."

Of course on most days he can only identify what he is feeling as "I'm mad" or "I am so angry." Therefore the first thing I do is show empathy, which is basically validating his feelings. I help him feel understood by saying something like, "It's normal to feel mad, it's okay to feel angry, Brennan. But now you have to choose what to do with those feelings."

My next question may be, "What did your brother do to make you mad?" to which Brennan might respond, "Cal won't play with me! He isn't being nice."

This is where we, as parents, have an opportunity to help our child identify the problem and begin to solve it. We can ask leading questions to help them get to the source of their emotions, such as, "Brennan, I sense that you are mad because Cal is reading a book rather than playing the game you want him to play. Are you feeling left out, or maybe Cal isn't giving you the attention you want? Do you think it's a good idea to hurt Cal with your hands and get disciplined, or should you talk to Cal and Mommy so we can come up with a plan? Let's come up with words to express how you feel."

Stop Your Words!

Another important lesson in self-control comes through teaching our kids how to "stop their words." When one of our kids begins to use hurtful or unkind words to express his frustration and anger, I will simply say something like, "Owen, stop your words! I need you to think about what you are saying, or what you are about to say, and choose wisely the way you want to express your feelings. You may tell me how you feel, but you may not attack your siblings or me with your words. Ask Jesus to help you keep your tongue from saying bad things."

In fact, we have memorized 1 Peter 3:10 (NLV): "If you want joy in your life and have happy days, keep your tongue from saying bad things and your lips from talking bad about others." So now I occasionally hear the boys quote, "Keep your tongue from saying bad things," to one another when they lack self-control with their words.

March Out the Mad

There are still plenty of days, however, that I'm sure our neighbors can hear any one of our boys emphatically declare, "I. Am. So. Mad." These are the times that I know they need more than just words to "get it out."

143

Therefore, another way we can train our children in self-control is by letting them physically express their emotions in a healthy way—the key word being *healthy*. I am not saying we should tell our kids to tear their room apart, kick the dog, or punch the walls. These are not healthy ways of expressing their frustration over an argument with their sibling. My directions tend to be more along the lines of, "Kids, jump on the trampoline and run ten laps around the house." Some days this helps, and other days, I tell them to run ten more. If nothing else, this exercise intrigues the neighbors. But you get the point. Just as adults benefit from physical exertion and exercise to relieve stress and tension, so do children.

Another helpful strategy to get your kids to physically express their anger or frustration is to get them to "march out the mad." This is a very useful tool when Owen is mad, or as he says it, "super mad." So some days you might look in our window and see Owen marching around the house, stomping his feet, swiftly moving his arms back and forth, and perhaps even producing a growl of some sort. But in due time, the march becomes a little less dramatic, Owen calms down, and soon thereafter he reengages in whatever it was he marched away from. He just had to physically get it out.

Calming Exercises

While Brennan and Owen tend to benefit most from expressing their frustration through physical activity, Cal tends to find his self-control through more calming exercises like counting and breathing. When Cal gets upset about something and cannot seem to regain his composure, I ask him to slowly count backwards from ten (or one hundred, if ten doesn't do the trick). He also finds self-control in taking ten long, deep breaths. There is something in the process of breathing in through the nose and out through the mouth that helps him think more clearly. This is always really helpful when Cal has a hard time letting go of the emotion he is experiencing even though he is no longer upset about the event or situation that led to the emotion.

One final and effective tool for helping our youngest ones gain self-control is by simply telling them to clasp their hands. The theory is that when your child is struggling with self-control, whether it's in the form of anger, focusing, or listening, clasping their hands redirects the energy into a concrete activity. The key word is redirect. Children can typically redirect the energy they were struggling to control into the purposeful task of clasping their hands, and in turn, exhibit self-control.

The Gift of Humor

Let us not forget the power of humor! Humor is often branded as an insufficient way of training our children because worn-out parents sometimes use it as an easy out when they can't bear another round of discipline and correction. Said simply, parents punt with humor. But the reality is humor can be a very effective tool for training our kids in self-control when used with purpose. Sometimes we must simply stop taking ourselves so seriously and remember the gift (and power) of laughter that God has given us. Injecting humor into a deteriorating scene between my kids with things such as "tickle monster" can be just what their hearts need. Or when the boys have a hard time letting go of the frustration they are feeling with one another, I tell them to get nose-to-nose for funny face time. My favorite is making them go toe-to-toe

> Sometimes we must simply stop taking ourselves so seriously and remember the gift (and power) of laughter that God has given us.

while singing "You Are My Sunshine" to each other. It's true, laughter is medicine for the soul.

In equipping our kids with these techniques, we are giving them some practical skills to respond rather than react and to live as men of knowledge who use words with restraint, and men of understanding who are even-tempered (Prov. 17:27). Our hope is that as they get older and have to make much tougher choices to exercise self-control, they will be equipped with the skills and knowledge to choose wisely, exercising the spirit of self-control that God gives them.

chapter 13
kindness

Be kind and compassionate to one another,
forgiving each other, just as in Christ God
forgave you.

—Ephesians 4:32

When I picked Cal up from his play date at the park, I asked, as usual, "How was your day, sweet face?"

Cal burst into tears. "Mom, someone called me weird on the playground, and he wouldn't let me play basketball with the group."

Seeing my sweet boy this upset made my mama bear instinct go into overdrive. I somehow mustered up the strength not to say what I wanted to say, which was along the lines of, "Baby, you can tell that kid that if he ever treats you that way again you will kick …" Well, never mind what I wanted to say. It completely lacked the compassion and kindness I long to model for the kids.

The world can be difficult and mean, but research reveals that children make seven times as many negative and controlling comments to their siblings as they do to their friends.[16] This research is just another reminder of how important it is to create a home where we are kind and compassionate toward one another so our home can be our haven. Our children know that we refuse to have a home where they tear each other down. Rather, our home is where we speak the truth in love. Paul said it so well in Ephesians: "Speaking the truth in love, we will grow to become in every respect the mature body of him who is the head—that is, Christ. From him the whole body, joined and held together by every supporting ligament, grows and builds itself up in love, as each part does its work" (Eph. 4:15–16).

We teach our children that God created us as a family for a purpose. He is not a God of "let's just let the pieces fall where they may." No, it was not by accident that God placed Cal, Brennan, and Owen in our care, and I want them to recognize how we are each an essential part of this family or "body." We teach our children that we are each growing into the person God created us to be, and each one of us has our own purpose to fulfill and work to do. If the children can grasp how they are each created with unique gifts and talents, they are more likely to celebrate one another's success. This is one of the ways we inspire kindness in, and among, the children.

Kindness Begins with Us

One wonderful way we can inspire kindness between our children is by modeling to them how to "encourage one another and build each other up" (1 Thess. 5:11). Each day, we can look for ways to build our children up with sincere words of love, affirmation, and affection. Ask yourself, "When I see my children after their long day at school, does my face light up and do my arms fly open?" Ask your children questions like, "Do you know how much I love being your mom? Do you know how much I enjoy being with you? Do you know how wonderfully and perfectly made you are?" One of the statements children most love to hear is, "I love watching you [blank]." You can fill in the blank, but the point is that children love hearing about the delight we find in watching them do what they love and be who they were created to be. It's not perfor-mance-based delight. It's not con-ditional delight. It's pure grace-indulgent delight. And for this reason, I love telling my boys how much pleasure I find in watching God work in their hearts (even when that means flushing out the sin) to fulfill his purpose for them.

> Ask your children questions like, "Do you know how much I love being your mom? Do you know how much I enjoy being with you?"

Kindness Leads to Repentance

Another great way to model kindness for our children starts with remembering that it is the kindness (not the wrath and harshness) of the Lord that leads to repentance. Oh, how quick I am to forget this truth in my parenting: "Don't you see how wonderfully kind, toler-ant, and patient God is with you? Does this mean nothing to you? Can't you see that his kindness is intended to turn you from your sin?" (Rom. 2:4 NLT).

I recall one afternoon when God used Brennan to make this truth finally resonate in my heart. While Brennan and Owen were sitting at the kitchen table color-ing, Brennan found it increas-

> It is the kindness (not the wrath and harshness) of the Lord that leads to repentance.

ingly difficult to share the crayons with his little brother. First, he didn't want to share the blue crayon, but it didn't take long for him to decide he didn't want to share any of the crayons with Owen. As the tension escalated between them, so did my frustration. And after several failed attempts to encourage our boys to think about how they could be kind and generous with one another, I came down on them pretty hard. My face was angry and my tone was harsh as I demanded new, kind hearts from them.

Brennan, in turn, reacted harshly to my little speech, and when I attempted to correct him for his tone, he responded with confusion. "But Mommy, that is how you just spoke to me."

I had just modeled the very thing I desired to eliminate, failing to remember that it is the kindness, not the harshness, of the Lord that turns us away from our sin. Yes, kindness and compassion are fundamental to a life lived in Christ, and they are a result of being forgiven in Christ. We give to others what we have freely received from Christ.

Are You Being Kind to One Another?

If you have spent any time at all in our home, you have heard me ask our children, "Are you being kind to one another?" Seems so simple, I know. But in asking this question, I am requiring the kids to really think about their actions and how those actions are affecting the other person.

And if I find our children walking a slippery slope toward a verbal outburst, another simple but effective question I ask is, "Are you building each other up or tearing each other down?" This question tends to stop them before they say something they will regret. Brennan has actually claimed this expression as his own. When Cal and Brennan are not getting along, it is not unusual to hear Brennan say, "Cal, why you wanna tear me down?" Awesome and not awesome. They are tearing each other down, but at least they are learning to identify it. That's progress, right?

When your children do tear each other down, have them give

thought to how they can build each other back up. Our kids have learned that if they say something harsh or hurtful, they will have to think long and hard about what they like about their sibling, and then speak those words of encouragement back into each other's hearts. They have to build each other back up, and they have to be specific.

Now let's be realistic—our children are naturally going to be competitive and experience conflict. It's part of the human experience. But in our family, tearing each other down is never tolerated, and it's always addressed. That is one way we address sibling rivalry and work to establish an atmosphere of kindness in our home.

Have Fun!

Another way we can model kindness and inspire it between our children is by having fun together as a family. It may sound trite, but extensive research reveals that a strong sibling relationship results from conflict being balanced with time spent enjoying each other and having fun together as a family.

Mom and Dad, enjoy your children! Spend quality time with them and tell them how much you enjoy their company. When we enjoy our children, we teach them that they are indeed enjoyable. This is yet another way we can reflect God's heart toward them—by reminding them how much God enjoys them and delights in their company.

If you have more than one child, find ways to squeeze in precious moments with each of them individually. Individual time is a tremendous gift we can give our children. Take your children on dates, doing the things that they enjoy doing. Even if the time you have is brief or simple, it will be something your child and you will cherish and remember.

You can turn even the most mundane times into special dates, even if it's just a macaroni-and-cheese lunch date at the kitchen table. This is what Brennan and I do on most days while Cal is at school and Owen is napping, and I make sure Brennan knows how much I enjoy this special one-on-one time with him (even on a day when all I can think about are the forty-seven other things I "should" be doing). Or I pick up Owen from preschool and I ask

> When we enjoy our children, we teach them that they are indeed enjoyable.

him where he'd like to take me on a lunch date. The pride that fills his face as he contemplates the special place he will take Mommy for lunch is priceless.

And I can't conclude my thoughts on taking your children on dates without mentioning the precious, and crucial, role that Dad plays. I am so thankful I'm married to a man who is also very purposeful in the way he models God's love and affection through his time with our kids. Although the golf course is calling his name, he has an incredible understanding of the invaluable role he has as their father and how much our kids need his presence in their lives. He gives them the most precious gift of all, his time and affection, and he makes sure they know they are the apple of Daddy's eye, just as they are the apple of the Lord's eye.

I just love the precious words of Psalm 17:8: "Keep me as the apple of your eye; hide me in the shadow of your wings." This verse doesn't read "make me" the apple of your eye; it says "keep me" as the apple of your eye. That means I already am the apple of God's eye. How amazing that makes me feel! Does your child know that he or she already is the apple of your eye and that nothing can change that? Enjoying them is the best place to start. And in doing so, don't be surprised when you see the kindness of the Lord flourish in their lives.

Comparing and Labeling

Just as we have to be intentional about the ways in which we inspire kindness in our kids, we have to be thoughtful about those things that incline our children to tear each other down and prevent them from showing kindness to one another.

An excellent book for understanding sibling rivalry is *Keep the Siblings, Lose the Rivalry* by Todd Cartmell, which offers very practical advice on how parents can be intentional in preventing sibling rivalry. One of the most valuable lessons I learned from this book is how destructive comparing and labeling can be in the sibling relationship.[17] Not only do labeling and comparing not build our children up; they wreak havoc in their souls. (This is useful information even for parents with one child, because it's common for a child to be labeled at school, among friends, or in various other venues.)

The most obvious and destructive form of labeling is words and actions that send the message to our children that they are unwanted or worthless. These labels not only break the heart of God, but they are the antithesis of the words God uses to describe his children. Therefore, if we must label our children, let us label them with the words God uses, such as *beloved, forgiven, precious, accepted, adored,* and *loved.*

> If we must label our children, let us label them with the words God uses, such as *beloved, forgiven, precious, accepted, adored,* and *loved.*

But even if we aren't using the harshest labels like *unwanted* or *unworthy,* there are other, much less obvious ways we might label our children, thereby humiliating them and distorting their sense of who they are in Christ.

For instance, comments like, "You are the smart one in our family,"

"You are the funny one in our family," and, "You are the trouble-maker in this family," are never helpful. You see, if Cal has been labeled the "smart one," we may begin to find Brennan trying to be particularly "wise." Or if Brennan is the "funny one," we may begin to see Cal become quite the prankster. And if we label any of our children a "troublemaker," we can rest assured he is likely to live up to that title and be exactly that, our little troublemaker.

Labels can also be limiting, even if the label is kind. For instance, if we tell Brennan he is our "athletic one" while we tell Cal he is our "smart one," Brennan may not be inclined to take his studies seri-ously because he has been told athleticism is his gift. Or Cal may never pursue certain sports because he has learned that such endeav-ors are for Brennan, the athletic one. And the likelihood that this kind of labeling builds resentment between them is high, very high.

Of course, you will be painfully aware of all the differences among your children. You will know which child tends to excel in school more easily than another, which child more easily attracts affection and attention from others, or which child seems to have more natural athletic ability. See, while we are indeed called to bring children up in harmony with their God-given talents and dispo-sition, there is a wise (and an unwise) way to go about this. And comparing and labeling one child as "more" anything than another does not foster kindness; it fosters only competition and resentment.

When Children Compare and Label Themselves

I was reminded how easily our children can claim a label as their own when my middle sister, Barbi, and her two boys came to Con-necticut for a weekend visit. We spent our first day at the pier, fish-ing, swimming, and diving off the dock. Brennan, who loves to keep up with his older cousins, was quick to swim out to the floating dock with them and take the first dive off the edge. Cal, on the other hand, stayed back on the pier to observe the fun, and I was never able to encourage him to join the boys. I tried, I desperately tried, but Cal was not going to budge. He decided that there were, as he said, "too many hungry fish in the ocean." He was apparently convinced that he would be dinner for a very small fish. In the meantime, we continued to celebrate Brennan's bravery for jumping off the dock.

The next day we returned to the dock for another day of summer fun. And again, Brennan took off for the floating dock with his older cousins while I stayed back on the pier with Cal and Owen. After numerous attempts to get Cal to dive into the water, he finally confessed what was in his heart. "Mommy," he said, "Brennan is the brave one, not me." I know that we never said, "Brennan is the brave one," but that didn't matter. That was the message Cal claimed as his own. When we celebrated Brennan's bravery, Cal became more aware of his fear.

Of course we did the right thing by celebrating Brennan's bravery; that wasn't the issue. What Cal taught me in this situation is something I had not previously understood: even when we don't label or compare our children, they may still feel the sting as they draw their own conclusions from the words they hear and the behavior they observe.

So the first thing I did was ask Cal to spend some time talking with me about all of the times, and in all of the ways, he has shown bravery. Examples did not come to his mind quickly, but we stayed with it, and together we identified many examples. So I praised Cal for the times he had shown courage in other situations, and I assured him of my confidence that he would swim (with the "hungry" fish) when he was ready. I also reminded Cal that this was the perfect opportunity for him to spur his brother on, to be proud of him for showing bravery.

But just as teaching our kids how to spur one another on in love and good deeds (Heb. 10:24) is important, it can be easy to confuse this kind of encouragement with the mistake of comparing.

Encouragement is: "Cal, I am so proud of you for learning how to read that book. I can tell you worked hard."

Labeling and comparing is: "Cal, you are our smart one! Brennan, I wish you would spend more time reading so that you can read as well as Cal."

Encouragement is: "Brennan, that song you made up was hysterical. You really made Mommy laugh with that one!"

Labeling and comparing is: "Brennan is the funny guy in our family. Cal, you should lighten up and be a little more fun like Brennan."

Let's not confuse the two, because while it is a beautiful thing to encourage and build up our children in God's love, we must be careful that in doing so, we are not tearing the other children down. Remember, to encourage and build each other up is to edify one another in the love and kindness of Christ. Or as Paul put it, "Do not let any unwholesome talk come out of your mouths, but only what is helpful for building others up according to their needs, that it may benefit those who listen" (Eph. 4:29).

Training in Kindness

To conclude my thoughts on kindness, I want to share one more story with you that illustrates the way kindness can take seed in our children's hearts through the example we set in reflecting the kindness of Christ to them.

As the only five-year-old on training wheels in our new neighborhood, Cal's confidence was taking a beating. He hadn't had much of an opportunity to hone his bicycling skills in our old neighborhood, but now it was time to get down to business. Mike gave him the "today is the day, son" talk, and they headed outside ready to conquer the world of bikes without training wheels. Every time Mike gave Cal the big push to send him off on his own, I watched with one eye open as he wobbled left, then right, and directly into a bush or curb. While Brennan and I nervously watched this all play out, Brennan made a point to remind me how much he really likes having training wheels on his bike. This was evidently not a situation in which he felt he needed to be exactly like his big brother.

It was no small feat, but over time, and with a lot of persistence and encouragement, Cal rode his little red bike, sans the training wheels, all the way down our street without a fall. And in that wonderful moment, I noticed Cal sit up a little straighter and hold his head a little higher. He was filled with pride. Equally as wonderful was the pride that Brennan had in his big brother. As Cal continued to ride up and down the street celebrating his newfound success, Brennan ran after him yelling, "Good job, Cal! Good job!" Cal overcame his fear, and Brennan celebrated his brother's success with a happy heart; he built him up! And we not only praised Cal for having the courage to ride his bike without training wheels but we also praised Brennan for showing the kindness of Christ to his big brother.

But let's be honest, real honest. Only thirty minutes later, when Brennan was feeling particularly feisty because he wasn't happy with the clothes I laid out for him for our evening plans, he pulled the "I'm leaving this family" card and marched to the front door, shoulders hunched and face scrunched. Simultaneously adorable and maddening!

Yes, kindness in our children, like all of the virtues we're talking

> Kindness in our children, like all of the virtues we're talking about, ebbs and flows. What does not ebb and flow is the kindness of Christ toward us.

about, ebbs and flows. What does not ebb and flow is the kindness of Christ toward us. How I love to be reminded of this.

Demonstrating the kindness of Christ, not only in the ways that we enjoy our children but also in the ways in which we teach them how to encourage one another in the love of Christ, is how we help them experience the wonderful kindness of Christ, the type of kindness that leads to repentance and faith.

chapter 14
thankfulness

*Rejoice always, pray continually, give thanks
in all circumstances; for this is God's will
for you in Christ Jesus.*

—1 Thessalonians 5:16–18

On October 29, 2012, Hurricane Sandy crashed into our little town. Thank God we were able to escape with the precious things like photo albums and baby journals, and most importantly, our safety. But much of the rest was swept away as fast as the tide came crashing in and out of our sweet little home.

The state of emergency began the night before Sandy hit. Our family of five bunked up with two other families in a house about thirty minutes inland. I remember curling up with a book that night called *One Thousand Gifts* by Ann Voskamp and thinking, "How fitting to be reading a book about thankfulness as I wait for the water to rise and pursue all my earthly treasure." I read each page slowly, not yet realizing that the kind of thankfulness Ann writes about was something I was going to need to hold on to in the days ahead.

Fast-forward twenty-four hours, after Sandy made her mark. We returned home to see the devastation. But as I looked around at all that was swept away and the little that remained, I was struck with the words I'd read in Ann's book just the night before: " 'On the night when he was betrayed, the Lord Jesus took some bread and gave thanks to God for it. Then he broke it in pieces' (1 Cor. 11:23–24). Jesus, on the night before the driving hammer and iron piercing through ligament and sinew, receives what God offers as grace (*charis*), the germ of His thanksgiving (*eucharistia*)? Oh. Facing the abandonment of God himself (does it get any worse than this?), Jesus offers thanksgiving for even that which will break him and crush him and wound him and yield a bounty of joy."[18]

I was reminded that *even then*, Jesus gave thanks (Luke 22:7–23). As I looked around me, I saw the water line on my mailbox that reminded me how high the water rose. I saw the house torn apart, the sea-kissed furniture, and the walls lined with water stains. But when I looked up, you won't believe what I saw. A rainbow painted in the sky. A rainbow that reminded me that God is faithful, he is good, and his promises are true. Ah yes, Jeannie, give thanks. And this heart of thanks is what carried us through the many months of tumultuous recovery to the other side of unimaginable joy.

Thankfulness Changes the Trajectory of Our Hearts

In a world of so much selfishness and entitlement, I really want to raise thankful children, ones who recognize that everything they are and everything they have is a gift from God. I want them to live in thankful awareness of the basics we take for granted, like a safe roof over our heads, healthy food to eat, clean clothes to wear, and safe water to drink. I want them to be thankful for all of the wonderful opportunities they are given, the places they get to go, and the experiences they enjoy. This is what I want—children who are thankful for everything God has given them.

But do you know what I want even more than children who are thankful for what they've been given? Children who are thankful for everything God has done for them. I want to foster in our children an overwhelming awareness of God's grace by teaching them what he has done for us by giving us Jesus. I want them to know, more than anything else, that because of God's great love for us, he sacrificed his one and only Son, for our sin, so that we can be reconciled with him through the atoning sacrifice of Jesus Christ. He loves us that much! While God has given us so much "stuff" to be thankful for, it pales in comparison with what he has done for us, and the gift he has given us in Christ.

Therefore, I want our kids to grow up with a thankfulness that is rooted in his wild and unfailing love for us. For this kind of thankfulness breeds gratitude, humility, generosity, and joy. And I never understood this more than after Sandy rocked our world.

God exhorts us to give thanks in all circumstances because he knows that thankfulness changes the trajectory of our hearts. It moves us from being focused on

> Thankfulness helps us see the rainbow, even in the ruin.

what we do not have and the long list of things that we want to all that has been given and all that is good. Thankfulness moves us from being focused only on ourselves to being focused on the needs of others. Thankfulness helps us see the rainbow, even in the ruin.

Thankfulness Is Learned

The human tendency is to look at everything we don't have and think, "Must have more!" Whereas the life we want to model for our

children is one where we look at what we have been given, be it much
or little, and say, "We are blessed." I want to model what the apostle
Paul teaches us in Philippians 4:8 and 12: "Finally, brothers and sisters,
whatever is true, whatever is noble, whatever is right, whatever
is pure, whatever is lovely, whatever is admirable—if anything is
excellent or praiseworthy—think about such things.... I know what
it is to be in need, and I know what it is to have plenty. I have learned
the secret of being content in any and every situation, whether well
fed or hungry, whether living in plenty or in want."

As demonstrated in these two verses, Paul understood from first-
hand experience several very important things. First, he understood
that what people allow to occupy their minds will infect their hearts,
and will determine their words and actions. So here Paul tells us to
allow the gospel of Jesus Christ to occupy our minds. Second, he
knew that union with the living Christ is the secret to being content.
And third, he understood that thankfulness is *learned*. Through his
trials and through his circumstances, Paul learned to live a life of
thankfulness.

To know whether we model for our kids the kind of life Paul
speaks of, we have to ask ourselves a few questions:

- Do we live our lives with open hearts and open hands, prepared to give of ourselves beyond what is easy and convenient,
  or are we obsessed with getting more, earning more, and having more at any cost?
- Do we worship the Giver of the gifts, or the gifts he has given?
- Do our children see in us radical self-interest and entitlement, or do they see us willing to freely give as we have freely
  received? (See Matt. 10:8.)

Indeed, our children are watching and learning thankfulness
through us. But even in our most unthankful moments, we need

not worry that all hope is lost. We can point our kids to Christ, who gave thanks and then gave his life for all of our unthankfulness!

Count Your Blessings

A fun way to encourage a "thankfulness outflow" is to play a simple game of "count your blessings." When the children are in one of those moods (you know the mood I'm talking about!) and the whining and complaining have taken over, we pause to play the game. Engaging your children in this game is as simple as asking each of them to name three or five (or ten!) things with which they have been blessed. More often than not, their unthankful spirit becomes thankful once again.

Giving thanks doesn't change our circumstances; it changes our hearts. It makes space for grace to fill the empty place, for thankfulness to have its rightful place in our hearts. Joy prevails when we give thanks.

> Giving thanks doesn't change our circumstances; it changes our hearts. It makes space for grace to fill the empty place, for thankfulness to have its rightful place in our hearts.

Another very practical way we can challenge our children is to simply ask, "Are you being thankful right now?" or, "Instead of complaining, can you tell me something you *are* thankful for?" You see, rather than telling our kids to be thankful, which we cannot force them to be, I invite them to think about that for which they are thankful. The goal is that they move out of the "I deserve more" mindset and instead focus on all that is good.

This is not to suggest that we don't allow our children to express disappointment or sadness, which is certainly a normal and in fact very necessary part of life. They need to be able to be honest with us about their disappointment. What is important is how they handle their disappointment. When they don't get their way, or they don't get the item they want from the checkout line at Target, or they don't get the first turn, do they become defeated and remain focused on their disappointment, do they pout and throw a fit, or can they refocus on all that is good and answer the question, "What *are* you thankful for?"

When our children get stuck and cannot answer that question, we have the wonderful opportunity to pause and ask them to join us in prayer—to ask God for thankful hearts that are rooted in his greatest gift of all, his Son.

Struggling with Selfishness

Entitlement and selfishness are the enemies of thankfulness. Based on my own struggle and experience with entitlement, I am determined to teach our children how easily selfishness can take seed in their hearts and steal their joy.

For example, Cal, as the oldest boy, is not unfamiliar with the conversation that begins with, "You are the leader. You must set a good example." This isn't to pressure or burden him but to encourage him in the role of leadership that God has given him with his brothers. And I am very much at peace with the example he sets, because he is a very strong, honest, and tenderhearted boy. He is so loyal with his love, particularly with his little brothers. However, I also recognize his tendency to have the "my way or the highway" attitude, just as I did at his age.

For instance, as I watched Cal play with four of his best buddies at our house, I noticed he would often insist that they play the game he wanted to play or tell each friend what to do and how to do it. It wasn't mean-spirited; it was just, well, bossy. When they did not follow his lead, and when they chose basketball over football, or jumping on the trampoline over looking at football cards, he quickly became frustrated.

I knew I needed to do something, but I didn't want to embarrass Cal in front of his friends, so I asked for his help in the kitchen so we could chat alone. I explained what I saw in his interactions with his friends, and I asked him why he was being so insistent on having his way. I reminded Cal that I understand what it feels like to struggle with selfishness, and we talked about what it means to be a good friend (to have good friends, you have to be a good friend) and the ways in which selfishness (being primarily concerned with one's own interests and wants) can isolate us in friendships. I also commended him for sharing so well, and I reminded him that sharing is something that good friends do with each other. I did not want him to walk away defeated, having only talked about what he was not doing well when indeed there were other things I could praise. At the end of our conversation, Cal recognized that he was not treating his buddies the way he would want to be treated, so we said a quick prayer and Cal committed to compromise and have fun doing the things that his friends wanted to do.

Think of Yourself Less

Cal is typically quick to recognize his wrongdoing and take responsibility for it. For that I am thankful. But the fact remains it's going to take time and commitment from Mike and me to help Cal inherit the wisdom we read in Philippians: "Do nothing out of selfish ambition or vain conceit. Rather, in humility value others above yourselves, not looking to your own interests but each of you to the interests of the others" (Phil. 2:3–4).

C. S. Lewis, in his awesome book *Mere Christianity*, frames this verse particularly well for our children. He writes, "True humility is not thinking less of yourself, but thinking of yourself less." What a powerful message for our children: think of yourself less often and think of Christ and others more. In other words, "Kids, when you are focused only on yourself—what you want, what you need,

> C. S. Lewis:
> "True humility is not thinking less of yourself, but thinking of yourself less."

and what you didn't get—you have no space left to be thinking about others. I am not telling you to think less of yourself. In fact, what I want is for you to see yourself through the eyes of Christ. I want you to understand your life in light of what Christ did for you. When you have a thankful heart that understands that everything you need you already have in Christ, you are free to put others before yourself and act in loving service toward those around you."

This is one of those areas, I believe, where actions speak louder than words. For example, while driving through a devastated neighborhood with only Brennan in the back seat, we came to a stop light where a homeless man was begging for money. I put the window down and waved the man over to us. As he walked toward our car, I opened my change compartment to grab spare change, but the only thing inside was a five-dollar bill. I'm embarrassed to admit, my selfish heart sank. I thought, "Oh no, now I have to give him a five-dollar bill. I was only going to give him spare change."

Knowing it was too late to change my mind, I said hello with a smile and put the five dollars in his cup. Can I just tell you, that man's face lit up with more joy than I have witnessed on another human's face in a very long time. Clearly overwhelmed, "Bless you, bless you," were the words he repeated as he walked away. My heart was now full and thankful. "No, bless *you*, bless *you*," I whispered, for reminding me that we are indeed happier when we give than when we receive.

After I put the window up, Brennan asked me why we gave our money to the homeless man, and God reminded me of the verse he wanted me to share with Brennan. "Well, baby, Jesus says, 'For sure, I tell you, because you did it to one of the least of My brothers, you have done it to Me' [Matt. 25:40 NLV]. So God just gave us an opportunity to love him by loving that beautiful man."

"That's so cool, Mom," my son said with a smile. And days later, Brennan was still talking about that encounter. Point being, my speech to my children about giving is good. My actions reflecting that speech are even better. But best is that in giving, God can turn our selfish hearts into thankful ones.

Jesus gives us so many examples of selfless love and humility, but I think the most beautiful example is found in John 13, where we find Jesus washing his disciples' feet at the Passover meal. With this simple but profound action, Jesus demonstrated extraordinary humility. Followers of Christ are called to emulate his attitude of selfless humility and love for others. Therefore, when we tell our children to exercise humility, we are challenging them to do away with self-seeking, self-important attitudes that steal our joy. We want their confidence rooted in the knowledge that they are each a beloved child of God, dearly and perfectly loved for who they are, not what they do, and they each have their own God-designed purpose. In this awareness, they are equipped to live in confidence *and* humility.

Give Rather Than Receive

A recent scenario in our home proved our boys are listening, and they are learning, about thankfulness. Brennan and Cal were playing with their new football cards, and I heard Brennan say, "Here, Cal, you can have this one, because I know you really like Tom Brady."

I couldn't believe my ears, quite frankly, so I joined the kids in the playroom and asked, "Brennan, did you just give Cal your new Tom Brady card?" (Brennan didn't have to reply because I now could clearly see the inexpressible joy on Cal's face.)

"Yup, I did, Mom," he replied.

"Wow, Brennan, that was really kind of you!" I said with a huge smile on my face. "Can you tell Mommy what made you decide to do that?"

Brennan replied, "Because we are happier when we give than when we receive, Mommy!"

Now of course this is not always Brennan's inclination. However, "We are more happy when we give than when we receive" (Acts 20:35 NLV) is a verse we have taught our children, so this particular situation with his brother was another awesome reminder that, indeed, the Word of God is alive and powerful and is able to occupy and transform our children's hearts. Let's admit it: being others-focused tends to be completely counterintuitive to most small children, and most adults for that matter. So it takes actually experiencing the "giving is better than receiving" lesson to help us understand the joy that flows from living selflessly and thankfully in Christ's footsteps. My prayer for my boys (and myself) is the same prayer that Paul had for his church in Colosse: "Let your roots grow down into him, and let your lives be built on him. Then your faith will grow strong in the truth you were taught, and you will overflow with thankfulness" (Col. 2:7 NLT).

My final thought on fostering thankfulness in our children lies in the giving not only of their time and talent but also of their treasure. When the boys recently earned ten dollars each for being extra big helpers to Mommy and Daddy during our move, they immediately began talking about what they might buy with their newfound riches. When they were done fantasizing about new Legos, football cards, and Mutant Ninja Turtles, we explained, "This is a good time to begin teaching you about what God tells us to do with the money he entrusts to us."

I could tell from the looks on their faces that they were already skeptical, perhaps fearful, of what we would say next.

"Boys," I continued, "the Bible tells us that where our treasure is, our heart will be also [Matt. 6:21], so it's our job to teach you how money is just another way we can worship God and put our trust in him. See, everything we have belongs to God, so before we spend that money, or save that money, we first give our tithe back to God. We need to think about how we can use the money God has given us to help those around us and reflect the extravagance of God's graciousness to us."

Once they finished asking wise questions about whether this is what Mike and I do with the money we earn, they agreed. God first.

In teaching our children that everything we are and everything we have is a gift from God, it is our great hope that they will experience the thankfulness and joy that flows from a life lived in Christlike selflessness and generosity, recognizing that everything they need they already have in Christ.

chapter 15

peacemaking

Live in peace with each other.... Make sure
that nobody pays back wrong for wrong,
but always strive to do what is good
for each other and for everyone else.

—1 Thessalonians 5:13, 15

While I was dressing Owen in his nursery, Brennan came bouncing in and proudly announced, "Mom, Cal just said poop!"

I turned to Brennan and my only response was, "And?"

Brennan looked surprised that I wouldn't know why he wanted me to know this important information. He replied, "Aaannnd ... Cal isn't allowed to say poop!"

"Brennan," I replied, "are you tattling to get Cal in trouble?"

"Nooo," Brennan assured me, "I just wanted you to know what he said!"

"Brennan," I asked again, "are you being a peacemaker or are you trying to get Cal in trouble?"

Brennan thought long and hard before he replied, "I'm trying to get Cal in trouble. Sorry, Mom."

"Brennan," I responded, "please go apologize to Cal for tattling on him and think about how you can be a peacemaker with your brother by encouraging him to make good choices." In other words, apologize to Cal for desiring to see him disciplined.

> A child of God is the beneficiary of his peace.

The kind of peace that Jesus gives cannot be found anywhere other than in fellowship with him. He gives us an inner rest of spirit that can't be obtained in any other way. A child of God is the beneficiary of his peace. And those who promote peace reflect the character of their heavenly Father. Or as Jesus put it, "Blessed are the peacemakers, for they will be called children of God" (Matt. 5:9).

Therefore, we explain to the children that a peacemaker is not someone who is fueled by arguing, getting even, and tattling. A peacemaker is, however, someone who strives to do what is good for the other. It is not someone who merely *feels* peace, but someone who pursues it. Consider Martin Luther King's definition of a peacemaker: "A peacemaker is someone who has sought to teach, to transform, to make friends, to heal, to defeat injustice, or to choose love instead of hate."

Prior to teaching our boys about being peacemakers, the word *peaceful* was not one you would have used to describe our home, probably because I was trying so hard to create a peaceful home but not relying enough on Jesus, the ultimate peacemaker, to provide it.

To teach our boys about the peace that comes from Christ, and how they can pursue peace in their relationships, we identified two main areas of focus:

1. Live in harmony with each other.
2. Develop good problem-solving skills.

I like to think of "living in harmony with each other" as conflict prevention, and "developing good problem-solving skills" as conflict resolution. By starting with conflict prevention, we minimize the need for conflict resolution!

Live in Harmony with Each Other: Conflict Prevention

One of my core texts for peacemaking is Philippians 2:13–16: "For it is God who works in you to will and to act in order to fulfill his good purpose. Do everything without grumbling or arguing, so that you may become blameless and pure, 'children of God without fault in a warped and crooked generation.' Then you will shine among them like stars in the sky as you hold firmly to the word of life."

This verse is an important reminder that it is God who works in you, not you who works in you, to act according to his good purpose. God works in us to make us "shine like stars in the sky" in a dark and sinful world, to be his love and light in this world.

Shine like stars in the sky? I like the sound of that. I mean, who doesn't want their children to shine like stars? Unfortunately, there was plenty of arguing and grumbling in our home, but not a whole lot of shining. So, to begin to teach our boys about peacemaking, we started with this message: "Boys, you are God's gift to each other. You may not always feel like a gift to each other, but you are. God gave you a best friend in your brother, and you are to build each other up in his love for you. He has made you a team, so invite God to work in your hearts to help you function as one."

TEAM—now that is a concept little ones can relate to.

- T: together
- E: everyone
- A: accomplishes
- M: more

Sounds silly, I know. But for some reason, it seems to hit home with little ones. And everyone knows, there is no arguing or tattling on a team.

When the children tattle on each other, I may ask them, "Are you delighting in your brother's suffering? Does it make you happy to see him disciplined?" Now of course the first time I asked Cal this question, he looked at me like I had two heads and asked, "I don't know, what is delighting, Mom?" But you get the point. I want them to reflect on their motive for tattling. Another great question to ask your children when they tattle is, "Please tell Mommy *why* you are telling on your brother [or sister] right now." This helps them think about the motive of their heart, and ultimately rethink tattling.

At times when one of our boys tattles, it is motivated purely by a desire to see his brother get in trouble, because nothing his brother said or did hurt him or made him sad. When he tattles, he is essentially saying, "Hey, Mom, I'm the good guy; he's the bad guy. I did not do anything wrong, and he did. That means I am great and he is not. Yay for me!" Pride and self-righteousness have reared their ugly heads, and it's up to me to help the tattler understand and recognize his own sin in his effort to point out another's (Matt. 7:3–5).

Other times kids tattle because one of them said or did something to the other that was unkind, either physically or emotionally. In both instances, we can train our kids how to work these things out between themselves to grow in their ability to be peacemakers.

For instance, our boys know that unless someone is hurt or in harm's way, I expect them to make peace before involving me. And if they are going to be peacemakers, they must develop good problem-solving skills to live in harmony with each other; they must learn conflict resolution.

Develop Problem-Solving Skills: Conflict Resolution

I don't know about you, but for the sake of my own sanity, I don't want to be involved in every detail of our children's disagreements. Not only that, but if we solve every disagreement for them, the only thing we teach them is to come to us every time there is a problem, so they learn very little in the process. Training them to be peacemakers means equipping them with the essential skills of problem solving. Studies consistently reveal that conflict between siblings is significantly reduced when problem-solving skills have been taught and demonstrated.

> Training children to be peacemakers means equipping them with the essential skills of problem solving.

Teaching our children to be peacemakers is also a precious opportunity to teach them about compromise and in turn to boost their self-confidence. I can always see the thrill on their faces when they successfully solve a problem they are having with each other. It's the look that says, "Hey, that felt good. I can do this!" In addition, they deepen the friendship and trust they have in each other, as Jesus said: "If a fellow believer hurts you, go and tell him—work it out between the two of you. If he listens, you've made a friend" (Matt. 18:15 MSG).

To help my kids learn peacemaking, I generally ask them a series of leading questions. While this kind of training can be intense for a time, be assured that the fruit of peace will be well worth the hard work of cultivation!

Ask: Did You Try to Solve the Problem Yourself?

The goal is that our children will be able to solve most of their arguments or disagreements without ever involving us. And to train our kids to accomplish this, the first important question we can ask our kids when they involve us in their argument is this: "Did you try to solve the problem yourself?"

Consider the following scenario:

Brennan: "Mom, Cal is watching a show on TV that we aren't allowed to watch."

Mom: "Did you attempt to solve this with Cal?"

Brennan: "Um, no."

Mom: "So what could you do now?"

Brennan: "I could tell Cal that we aren't allowed to watch this show."

Mom: "Good idea, Brennan. Perhaps you can also encourage Cal to make a good choice and change the channel. If he does not listen, you may ask for my help, but first try to work it out together. See if you can be a good friend and help him make a good choice."

In asking, "Did you try to solve the problem yourself?" you are essentially asking your child to think about what a peacemaker would do.

Ask: What Can You Do Now?

However, if the kids are not successful at solving their problem without us, we can ask a series of questions that still allows *them* to solve the problem. We can walk our children through this kid-friendly problem-solving process without having to do any of the problem solving ourselves. Yes, they need direction and guidance with this approach, but with a little practice and persistence, they are off and running on their own, as in the following example.

Cal: "Mom, Brennan took my football card, and when I tried to get it back, he pushed me."

Mom: "Did you try to work this out with Brennan first?"

Cal: "Yes, but he pushed me."

Mom: "What do you think you could do now?"

Cal: "I don't know, Mom. I need your help."

Mom: "How did you try to work it out with Brennan?"

Cal: "I grabbed the card out of his hand and yelled at him for taking it. Mom, it's mine!"

Mom: "Can you think of a better way you could have handled that? Perhaps you can tell Brennan that it's not kind to take things from each other without asking and that he needs to give you your card back and ask you for permission to borrow it when you are done with it."

Cal: "But he pushed me too!"

Mom: "I heard you tell me that you yelled at him. Do you think that perhaps you both have made some hurtful choices that you need to apologize for? Can you try again to work it out with the skills Daddy and I have taught you? Invite God to work in each of your hearts and help you work together as a team to make this right. If that does not work, please let me know and I will help you, but rest assured there will be consequences if I have to get involved. I have confidence in you guys to solve this problem without me."

Asking questions like, "What could you do now?" and, "How could you have handled the situation differently?" requires them to reflect on what happened and why they came to me, because even when they "think" they have attempted to solve the problem, they may not have given it much effort. Therefore, I immediately put it back in their hands. Asking questions requires your child to think through their options (and seek God's help) before relying on you to solve their problem. It is only when they get stuck in solving the problem without me that we progress to the following steps.

Ask: What Is the Problem, and How Do You Feel?

I ask both children to state what happened by identifying the problem or incident that occurred as well as the feeling that resulted. I also ask them to start their sentences with *I* because then they cannot start by pointing the finger. This also allows them to identify the role that they played in the situation and if/how they contributed to the problem.

Perhaps Cal's response will be, "I was playing with my football card and Brennan took it," and the feelings that resulted will be, "I got angry and yelled." Then Brennan has an opportunity to do the same. Perhaps Brennan's response will be, "I took the card from Cal because he wasn't using it anymore and I really like it," and his resulting feelings will be, "I am mad because it's not fair that Cal won't share."

Ask: How Can You Solve the Problem?

Now that both children have heard the other's version of the problem and the feelings that resulted, I ask both children to think about what a peacemaker would do and how we can solve the problem. Sometimes I even take the toy away and send them to their room (which they share) to come up with a plan. I let them know that they can return to me only after they have figured out how to solve this problem and better share their toys. But until then, they must stay in their room and the toy stays with me.

If I don't send them to their room to solve the problem together, I allow them each to state how they think we can solve the problem. If all goes according to my nice little plan, Brennan will say, "I shouldn't have taken the card away from Cal. I didn't treat him the way I would want to be treated. I was thinking only about myself. I will wait till Cal is done." But if it doesn't all go according to my nice little plan (which is typically the case), Brennan may say, "He's just keeping the card because he knows I want it. He's not a nice brother, and I'm not going to share any of my stuff with him either."

What I am learning through the solutions they come up with is that the stated problem is rarely the real problem. As was the situation in this case, the solution was a lot less about the card and a lot more about two specific things. First, it was about feeling wronged by the other person. Second, it was about an attitude of "I want what I want when I want it, and it doesn't matter what you feel or think." It's about the belief behind the behavior!

So here we have a precious opportunity to encourage our kids to think about what's going on in their hearts, and the solutions that we choose for a peaceful resolution must address this.

Ask Leading Questions to Come to a Peaceful Resolution

Seeking a peaceful resolution is where you really have the opportunity to teach them about compromise, teamwork, and empathy. I may ask, "Brennan, how do you feel when Cal takes a toy from you? Would you like it if Mommy allowed him to keep something he took from you?" Or, "Cal, how do you feel when Brennan yells at you when you do something he doesn't like? Is there a better way you could have communicated your frustration with him?"

Through leading questions such as these, the children can usually come to a peaceful solution, such as "Cal can have his card back, and he will share it with Brennan when he is done using it. And we will use our words instead of our hands, and speak with kindness, even when we are frustrated with each other." I'm sure it won't surprise you to hear that when Cal is done playing with the football card, Brennan is typically no longer interested in it, because it is rarely about the object in dispute to begin with.

In this process, our children will learn how to practice patience, pursue peace in their relationships, and develop problem-solving skills that help them become makers of peace. And more importantly, our prayer is that they will be reminded of the true source of our peace, as we read in Isaiah 26:3, "You will keep in perfect peace those whose minds are steadfast, because they trust in you."

chapter 16
honesty

*The LORD detests lying lips, but he delights
in people who are trustworthy.*
—Proverbs 12:22

I clearly remember a time in my life when I was told to lie about my age. A family friend took my best buddy, Robert, and me to the zoo. As we pulled up to the entrance and prepared to purchase our tickets through the car window, Robert and I were told to pretend we were only five years old so that we could get in for free. We all laughed and celebrated the fact that we saved ten dollars, but something inside (you could call it the Holy Spirit) told me it wasn't really all that funny, and I knew it didn't feel right.

This experience from my childhood is such an important reminder for me now. Let us not underestimate our children's sense of right and wrong. The Holy Spirit convicts young and old hearts alike.

Honesty is, no doubt, an essential virtue to teach our kids. The big question is, How do we explain such a deeply complex virtue to little children? How do we help them understand that *honesty* is a lot more than simply *not lying*?

Honesty is described in the dictionary with words such as *truthfulness, integrity,* and *sincerity.* But there are other, much more poignant synonyms that came to mind as I really began to delve into the depths of honesty—the primary two being *authenticity* and *vulnerability.*

Being an authentic and vulnerable person means that we do not create a false image of perfection, particularly to our children. It means that we allow our kids to see the "realness" of who we are and our desperate need for a Savior. Yes, authenticity, expressed through vulnerability, is the genuine characteristic of an honest person—a person who understands the power of grace!

Now I know some parents who fear that if they allow their child to see their weakness and sin—if they are authentic with their kids—their children may not respect them as they ought. I think it's quite the contrary. When we are honest and authentic with our children about our own sin, they will actually begin to understand the power of God's forgiveness through our example. It will fix their eyes on Jesus, and the freedom that he purchased for us on the cross. It will fix their eyes on his grace.

> When we are honest and authentic with our children about our own sin, they will actually begin to understand the power of his forgiveness through our example.

However, if I, as a parent, am duplicitous and disingenuous in my relationship with my children—that is, if I am one kind of person at one time and another kind of person at other times—they will quickly learn to imitate a double standard of behavior.

Therefore, to teach the virtue of honesty to our children, we must teach and model how to live an authentic life. Anything less leads to a life entangled in sin and hindered from the freedom that Christ purchased for us on the cross. As we read in Hebrews 12:1–2, "Let us throw off everything that hinders and the sin that so easily entangles. And let us run with perseverance the race marked out for us, fixing our eyes on Jesus, the pioneer and perfecter of faith."

Little White Lies

There is great truth in the expression "Oh what tangled webs we weave when first we practice to deceive." I recently had to confront this truth in a situation with Cal. We were planning a weeklong trip to Atlanta, and Cal was going to miss five days of school. Since we had already received the "your son has missed too many days this year, please make school a priority" letter, I knew this trip was not going to go over well with his school. As I pondered whether to call him in sick for the week (What's the harm in that? We won't be hurting anybody with that little white lie), I realized I would need to tell Cal to lie to his teacher. I would teach Cal that honesty is conditional and integrity can be compromised for matters of convenience. So I chose the truth.

Let us not be fooled; our children learn from our example. If we are dishonest with, or for, our children, we teach them that honesty is conditional. They begin to ask, "If Mom and Dad can be dishonest in certain situations, why can't I?" As parents, we have to ask ourselves, "Is this little white lie worth the lesson I am teaching my child? Am I modeling the honest life Jesus calls us to live?"

> If we are dishonest with, or for, our children, we teach them that honesty is conditional.

Of course there will be times when we must protect our children from information that may be harmful to them and we must be very careful with the truths we offer them. Their little ears are not prepared for most of the realities of this world, so please understand I'm not suggesting we tell them everything there is to know when they ask a question that they are not mature enough to handle. We have to be wise with the "need to know" basis. This kind of protection we must provide for our children is very different than being dishonest out of convenience.

You know the kind of dishonesty I'm talking about. Rather than telling our children they cannot play with a certain toy, we tell them it's broken. If we don't want to take them to McDonald's, we tell them it's closed. Instead of teaching them how to deal with *no* and disappointment, we fabricate a convenient alibi.

Keep Thinking

Teaching our children about little white lies can be sticky business. We learned this lesson the hard way. When my mom, whom the boys call Goggi, recently came for a visit, she arrived excited to share a few gifts she had purchased for the boys. They could tell from the shape of the package that Goggi had brought new books, which they know is her favorite gift to give. Thankfully the boys love books, so they excitedly ripped off the wrapping paper, only to find books Cal was not excited to receive. Rather than show thankfulness for the gift, Cal dropped his head, left the book on the floor, and walked back outside to continue his game of basketball.

Mortified, I followed Cal outside fully prepared to give him my "be thankful" lecture, but I stopped just long enough to ask, "Cal, what was that all about?"

"Mom," he replied, "I don't like the book she gave me, so I wasn't going to lie and tell her I did."

Okay, talk about a teachable moment for both of us. This is where we came up with another family mantra: "If you don't have anything nice to say, *keep thinking*." Rather than tell a little white lie, we can keep thinking until we have something kind to say while also telling the truth.

I explained, "Cal, I am not asking you to tell a little white lie to Goggi and pretend you like the book she gave you, but there is certainly something kind you could have said to show thankfulness for being given a gift. That in and of itself is a wonderful thing." Together, in this teachable moment, we did come up with some honest but kind things he could have said if he had "kept thinking."

Tell the Truth, Even When It's Difficult

Mike has an expression he has long used with the children, which is, "Tell the truth, even when it's difficult." I find myself using this phrase often to remind our kids that honesty is not circumstantial in our family.

For example, when I picked Cal up from school, he slowly stepped into the car with an "I know I'm in trouble" look on his face. He wasn't his usual energetic "Hi, Mom!" self. When I asked him what happened at school, he responded, "You already know, Mom. My teacher told me she sent you an email."

I responded, "Well, yes, she did, but I would like to hear it from you. And Cal, we tell the truth, even when it's difficult, right?"

Cal proceeded to explain how he was caught daring his buddy to kiss a little girl on the playground, and as a consequence for his misbehavior, his teacher had him stack the chairs at the end of the day. When Cal was done telling me what happened, I asked him to explain to me what was wrong with what he'd done. Then we talked about the importance of showing girls respect. I also asked Cal if there was anything inside of him that made him feel like he was not making a good choice, to which he replied, "I knew it was wrong, Mom, but I was making people laugh, so I did it anyways."

Here I was given the precious opportunity to talk to Cal about the "Holy Spirit nudge." Unfortunately, I didn't do it. I was too focused on the behavior Cal had displayed rather than the work God wanted to do in his heart. It wasn't until I told my sister this story about Cal, and she asked, "Did you talk to him about the 'Holy Spirit nudge'?" that I realized my missed opportunity. Just as God used the Holy Spirit to convict Cal in that moment on the playground, he used my sister to convict me in this situation. And it was a powerful reminder that teaching our kids about Christlike character is not about making them obey but about reaching their hearts so that God may reveal his truth and grace to them.

So now when Cal tells me he did something he knew in his heart he shouldn't have done, my prayer is that I will remember to talk about the ways in which the Holy Spirit works in us and through us to make us more like Jesus, to remind Cal about the ways in which the Holy Spirit convicts, comforts, empowers, and guides us in God's will for our lives. While it all may be too much for my sweet eight-year-old to fully grasp, I am at least able to help Cal identify moments in his life when he experiences the "Holy Spirit nudge."

> It's important that we do acknowledge and praise wise and honest choices, even when dishonest and unwise ones precede them.

But back to what I did do, the way I did handle the playground incident.

After Cal and I finished discussing the ways in which he could have behaved, Cal asked, "So what is my consequence, Mom?" The first thing I did was praise him for his honesty. I believe it's important that we do acknowledge and praise wise and honest choices, even when dishonest and unwise ones precede them. If God delights in people who are truthful, I too want to delight in my children when they choose the truth. I appreciated his honesty about the situation, and I wanted to make sure he knew how proud I was that he chose to tell the difficult truth.

The next thing I did, to his great pleasure, was let him know that I was not going to give him any further consequences. I explained that because his teacher already gave him a consequence in the classroom, because he took accountability for what he did, and because he showed genuine remorse for his sin, I was going to show him mercy, just as Christ loves to show us mercy.

When the children choose to tell the truth, take accountability for their actions, and show sincere sorrow for their sin, their consequence tends to be much less severe. This is not to suggest that they do not receive consequences when they are honest; I just tend to show more mercy when they are. I like to believe I am giving them opportunities to experience the freedom that comes in choosing truthfulness and integrity.

Lying out of Shame and Fear

Interestingly enough, research reveals, "increasing the threat of punishment for lying only makes children hyperaware of the potential personal cost. It distracts the child from learning how his lies impact others. In studies, scholars find that kids who live in threat of punishment don't lie less. Instead they become better liars, at an earlier age—learning to get caught less often."[19]

But what about those times when our children choose to be dishonest, or what if they tell only the partial truth? What if Cal had not taken responsibility for his actions or blamed another child for what he chose to do? These are the times, I believe, when our children allow fear and shame to dictate their response. They know they did something wrong and they are ashamed of it, or they know they did something wrong and they are afraid of the consequences they will receive. They may want to be honest, but fear of punishment or disappointing us interferes.

The problem is our children cannot fully appreciate what this does to their hearts, so they lie, thinking this will be the easier way out. And they forget that even when we may not know of their sin or wrongdoing, God does. Ultimately, they are accountable to him. So we want our children to feel inclined to confess their sin because they can trust there is a Savior who has already forgiven it.

I'd like to share a story with you to illustrate the way our children seek to simultaneously avoid consequences and please us, even if it means choosing dishonesty.

It was a beautiful summer day. The kids were having a blast in the bouncy castle, and I was relaxing in the hammock my sweet husband had just given me for Mother's Day. However, my bliss was quickly interrupted when Cal announced, "Hey, Mom, check out Brennan!"

I looked over my shoulder to find Brennan going potty in our neighbors' bushes. Little did I realize that when Brennan told me he needed to go potty and I replied, "Well, baby, then go to the potty," that he would use the nearby hydrangea bush!

Concerned our new neighbors were watching in disgust, I ran to his side and asked, "Brennan, what did you just do?"

Brennan pulled his pants up and sheepishly replied, "Will you be mad if I tell you I just went potty in the neighbors' yard?"

> We want our children to feel inclined to confess their sin because they can trust there is a Savior who has already forgiven it.

I couldn't help but smile at his response. He wanted to tell the truth but he was afraid of punishment and disappointment. Often, children will lie to make you happy, to try to please you. So if they realize that the truth is what pleases you, and not just hearing good news, they will be more motivated to tell the truth, even if it's a painful truth. And this is also how we get to the heart of the issue and help our children understand why we are prone to dishonesty.

This is why my response to Brennan's question, "Will you be mad?" was, "Brennan, I don't want you to worry about whether I will be mad. I don't want you to think about pleasing me. I want you to be honest so you don't carry the guilt that comes with lying. And I want you to remember that whatever you did wrong has already been forgiven and paid for in Jesus. Ask God to give you a heart that desires honesty. You are free to tell the truth." And this led to a little conversation about how we reap what we sow.

Reaping What We Sow

Paul taught the universal law of consequences: "Do not be deceived: God cannot be mocked. A man reaps what he sows. Whoever sows to please their flesh, from the flesh will reap destruction; whoever sows to please the Spirit, from the Spirit will reap eternal life" (Gal. 6:7–8).

For instance, when we sow seeds of dishonesty and insincerity, we will reap a harvest of mistrust, guilt, and hypocrisy. I'm not referring to the karmic "what goes around comes around" system of payback, which is in complete contradiction to grace, but simply acknowledging that our choices do indeed have consequences. Even if we escape the worldly ramifications of a certain situation, our spirits know the truth. And little by little, the choices we make will either edify or wreak havoc in our souls (Mark 8:36). Disingenuous living reaps disastrous results.

Every parent knows the importance of teaching our children that there are consequences to their actions. But when we teach this reality to our kids, it's even more important for our children to understand another truth: Simple cause and effect in our human interactions is not true of our life before God. God is not keeping score and ensuring that the consequences flow in direct proportion to the offense. As we read in Psalm 103:8–10, "The LORD is compassionate and gracious, slow to anger, abounding in love. He will not always accuse, nor will he harbor his anger forever; he does not treat us as our sins deserve or repay us according to our iniquities."

So I explained to Brennan, "Even when Mommy or Daddy doesn't know the truth about what you've said or done, you do. And when you're not honest and you keep secrets stored up in your heart, you carry a burden Jesus doesn't want you to carry. When you feel bad or yucky or embarrassed about what you've said or done, that's called guilt and shame for your sin. But Jesus has already paid the price for whatever you said or did that you are hiding in your heart. So while you may have consequences from Mommy and Daddy because it's important for us to teach you how to live, Jesus has already forgiven you. You are free to be honest with us and with Jesus" (Rom. 8:1).

When our children sow to please the Spirit by putting their trust in God and seeking to honor him through a life of authenticity, they experience the freedom of having peace of mind, they generously reap the benefits of having a trusting relationship with Mike and me, and most importantly, they feel at peace with God.

chapter 17

in him and
through him

My body and my heart may grow weak,
but God is the strength of my heart
and all I need forever.

—Psalm 73:26 NLV

A few hours after I had a little conversation with Brennan about relying on the Holy Spirit to help him with his temper, Brennan returned to me and proudly announced, "Mom, I got it! I finally figured out who the Holy Spirit is!"

"Awesome, Brennan! I want to hear all about it!" I said with a smile as I knelt down and looked into his eyes, wanting him to know what a special moment this was.

"Well, Mom," Brennan explained, as he looked at me as though he couldn't believe it had taken this long for it to click in his mind. "God is the Father. And Jesus is the Son. And the Holy Spirit is the baby!"

It appeared we had some more explaining to do! But my heart was full with the knowledge that Brennan was trying to understand the great gift God has given us in the Holy Spirit and the power that comes from living "in him and through him." Though our young children may not fully comprehend how the Holy Spirit is *Jesus*, the very *spirit of Jesus*, or the *conviction* and *comfort* that the Spirit brings, it's never too early to begin planting the seeds.

The Trinity and the Holy Spirit

Our children's pastor explains the Holy Spirit to our children through the classic egg analogy. He explains, "The egg is God. And when you split the egg, you find three parts total—yolk, egg white, and the shell. All three parts are God, but each one has its own unique attributes. The Holy Spirit is the helper and that's the part of God with us now. Another way to explain the three-in-one of the Trinity is through an analogy with water. God symbolizes the water, and water exists in three distinct forms: liquid (tap), solid (ice cubes), and gas (steam)."

Of course, no analogy is perfect because God cannot adequately be compared to anything, but it gives our children a glimpse of understanding into the Holy Spirit, who is not like anything we know or see. Such a marvelous mystery. What *is* important for our children to understand is that the Holy Spirit is the part of the Trinity that lives with us and in us. He helps us know what is right and wrong, guides us in truth, and empowers us (John 16:13–15).

Therefore, as we talk about the Holy Spirit with our kids, we

> Though our young children may not fully comprehend how the Holy Spirit is *Jesus*, the very *spirit of Jesus*, or the *conviction* and *comfort* that the Spirit brings, it's never too early to begin planting the seeds.

can teach them how impossible it would be to try to live like Christ without the power of Christ. We can encourage them by teaching them that they do not need to seek to live like Christ in their own strength, but that Jesus has given them an *advocate* (a helper) in the Holy Spirit. As Jesus said, "If you love me, obey my commandments. And I will ask the Father, and he will give you another Advocate, who will never leave you. He is the Holy Spirit, who leads into all truth" (John 14:15 – 17 NLT).

From my own personal experience, I can say with confidence that teaching our children about growing in the likeness of Christ can all too easily creep from "in him and through him" to "Here is your checklist for obeying God's commands to become more like him. Do more, try harder, and be better!" Unfortunately, this type of legalistic approach to growing in his likeness will only create a disdain for God and a deeply misguided notion that we can earn God's favor or acceptance by keeping the rules. This approach inevitably leads to disobedience and defeat, because it suggests that God conducts "performance evaluations" to determine our worthiness.

So at the risk of sounding redundant, but knowing how much our souls need to be refreshed with the gospel over and over again, let's briefly explore how we can keep the focus on the power of the Holy Spirit as we teach our kids about "growing in Christlike character."

We Are Weak but He Is Strong

One of the key components to parenting a wholehearted child is raising our children's awareness of just how weak and incompetent they are in their flesh and just how strong and competent Jesus is for them. As we said in the first chapter, this means that we want our children to grow up with a keen awareness of just how wholly dependent they are on Jesus to be for them what neither they nor anyone else (we parents included!) can ever be.

> The Christian life is grounded not in how good and strong I am for God but in how good and strong Christ was (and is) for me.

The worst thing we could do to our children is train them to think that in and of themselves, they are strong and self-sufficient. Conversely, the best thing we can do for our children is to help them know that "they are weak but he is strong." The Christian life is grounded not in how good and strong I am for God but in how good and strong Christ was (and is) for me. As we grow in our understanding of the gospel, we don't see this as bad news but as life-giving truth. In my keen sense of awareness of my weaknesses, I am reminded of the one who is my perfection, and how very much I need him, as Paul so beautifully illustrates in Romans 7:

> What I don't understand about myself is that I decide one way, but then I act another, doing things I absolutely despise.... For if I know the law but still can't keep it, and if the power of sin within me keeps sabotaging my best intentions, I obviously need help! I realize that I don't have what it takes. I can will it, but I can't *do* it.... My decisions, such as they are, don't result in actions. Something has gone wrong deep within me and gets the better of me every time. It happens so regularly that it's predictable. The moment I decide to do good, sin is there to trip me up. I truly delight in God's commands, but it's pretty obvious that not all of me joins in that delight.... I've tried everything and nothing helps. I'm at the end of my rope. Is there no one who can do anything for me? Isn't that the real question? The answer, thank God, is that Jesus Christ can and does.
>
> —Romans 7:15–25 MSG

When I live in the truth that Jesus Christ can, and does, cover me with his perfect righteousness, and his love and acceptance of me are not based on my ability to do my best, some wonderful things begin to happen: I am set free from the judgment of others (not to mention self-judgment), I am set free to display the excellence of his grace in my life, and I am set free to pursue excellence in the life that he has given me. And when I fail, which I often do, I can rest in the assurance that my life is hidden in Christ, so when God looks at me, he first sees the righteousness of Jesus covering me (Col. 3:3).

Knowing that "I can't but he can" opens me up to living exactly how I was created to live—in him and through him. There is hope, and respite, and strength when we do life through the inexhaustible power of the Holy Spirit. And as a result, we use the gifts and talents he has given us to bless others and bring him glory.

Pleasing God

When Mike and I met with Cal's teacher for an end-of-the-year debriefing, we were reminded that Cal is a child who needs to be encouraged to fulfill his potential. His teacher said, "It's all in there. Cal is very bright, but he needs to focus much more to fulfill his potential." The problem is Mike and I cannot make our children fulfill their potential. They need to want it, whatever "it" may be, more than we want it for them.

What we can do is spur our children on by encouraging them to rely on Jesus. We can help them see the possibilities that lie within the unique gifts God has given them. We can teach our children about the stories in the Bible where God multiplied and blessed the people who used, rather than wasted or hid, the gifts God had given them. We can talk to them about the Holy Spirit who equips us with everything needed to do the work God calls us to do. And finally, we can remind them how much delight Jesus finds in their desire to trust him with the gifts he has given them. "We ask God to give you complete knowledge of his will and to give you spiritual wisdom and understanding. Then the way you live will always honor and please the Lord, and your lives will produce every kind of good fruit. All the while, you will grow as you learn to know God better and better" (Col. 1:9–10 NLT).

Now we have to tread carefully here, because we do not want to risk suggesting to our children that we earn God's pleasure through our obedience, our excellence, or our "best-ness." God is pleased by our trust and faith in him, and he is pleased by our obedience when our obedience is a result of that faith and trust in his love for us (Heb. 11:6). There is no pleasing God independent of our faith and trust in Jesus. God is pleased with us when his grace and power are evidenced and glorified through our lives in him. What's important for our children to understand is that they are absolutely, completely, and wholeheartedly loved and accepted in Christ because of his finished work for them on the cross. Accepting *that* gift pleases him.

> There is no pleasing God independent of our faith and trust in Jesus. God is pleased with us when his grace and power are evidenced and glorified through our lives in him.

God Is Our Strength

In teaching our children about living "in him and through him," I am not underestimating the importance of teaching our kids about being strong and courageous. Of course these are monumentally important things for our kids to understand, and Deuteronomy 31:6 underscores this importance: "Be strong and courageous. Do not be afraid or terrified.... for the LORD your God goes with you; he will never leave you nor forsake you."

But our strength and courage are not rooted in our own feeble efforts to "muster up what it takes." Pulling ourselves up by our bootstraps works only until our bootstraps break. See, God is not only our refuge. He is also our strength (Ps. 46:1). As Christians, we can be strong and courageous, trusting in Christ's strength, not our own. We can trust that even when we can't keep holding on to him, he keeps holding on to us. Likewise, we want our chil-

> **We can trust that even when we can't keep holding on to him, he keeps holding on to us.**

dren to feel confident in the knowledge that God will give them the strength and courage to climb any mountain he gives, or allows, them to climb: "I have strength for all things in Christ Who empowers me [I am ready for anything and equal to anything through Him Who infuses inner strength into me; I am self-sufficient in Christ's sufficiency]" (Phil. 4:13 AMP).

For example, when Brennan turned three, his mantra became "I can't, I can't." I think this was when he became painfully aware of all the things his big brother (his hero) could do, and all the things he so desperately wanted to be able to do, but couldn't.

Swimming lessons for Brennan brought the "I can't, I can't" front and center. Fear was written all over his face as we walked through the front doors of the YMCA on the way to his first swimming lesson. But before I sent Brennan off to meet his swim instructor, we sat down on the bench and had a quick conversation about fear. I said, "Brennan, you can do this. You are a very brave boy, Mommy is here cheering for you, and God can give you the courage you need. Baby, rely on God's courage in you, and don't let fear win!"

I could tell it was the "rely on God's courage in you" that hit home because with that, he jumped in the pool and exclaimed, "Fear, you are going down!"

Ephesians 6:11 is another great verse for encouraging our children to be bold in God's strength: "Put on the full armor of God, so that you can take your stand against the devil's schemes." Can't you just see a little child playfully and boldly proclaiming, "I've got my armor on, Mom!" And while they cannot fully appreciate what God's *full* armor is (the belt of truth, breastplate of righteousness, gospel of peace, shield of faith, helmet of salvation, and sword of the Spirit), there is plenty of time for them to learn how it allows them to take their stand against the devil.

Please know I'm not one to lightly toss around the word *devil*. Our children, however, are at an age where they are certainly becoming aware of good and evil in this world. We don't do our children any favors by pretending evil doesn't exist; as 1 Peter 5:8 warns, "Stay alert! Watch out for your great enemy, the devil. He prowls around like a roaring lion, looking for someone to devour" (NLV). Therefore, when the children have questions about the devil, we simply explain, "God loves you, and he is for you. His desire is to bless you with his love, and his peace, and his joy. But the devil, well, he is jealous of God's greatness. His purpose is to destroy us and tempt us away from the life that God wants us to experience. He wants us to doubt God's goodness and grace. The devil does not want you to be strong and courageous. He does not want you to fulfill the purpose for your life. But with God's armor, you do not need to fear. Jesus, in you, has already won the victory."

I'm certainly not pretending that this kind of speech always works. There are plenty of days when "in him and through him" does not translate to our children, and their fear, laziness, or sense of defeat prevail (just as *my* fear, laziness, and sense of defeat often prevail!). I have found that in times such as these, the best thing we can do is remind our kids that Jesus knows and understands how they feel. We can continue to encourage them to rely on Jesus as their source of comfort and strength.

Dealing with Failure

You see, at some point, if not already, our children will learn that life is not a walk in the park. In fact, on most days, it's not even a casual jog. We all struggle and suffer, sometimes in very small ways, and sometimes in monumental ways. When our children declare, "Life isn't fair," because their brother got a bigger scoop of ice cream or because they didn't get chosen at recess to be on the kickball team, we can affirm their feelings with, "You're right, honey. Life isn't always going to be fair." In fact, some of the most truthful advice we can give our kids is that life is not fair and life is not easy, and most often, it's the hard and unfair things that shape us. But the good news is we can assure our children that grace defeats unfair every time. If anyone could have pulled the "it's not fair" card, it was Jesus. But instead, he endured the cross and exchanged his perfect righteousness for our sin and shame so he could meet us in the unfair places and empower us to live in the truth of his grace.

While we may not have control over what happens to us, we do have a say in how we respond and allow it to shape us as we turn to God in our need. So when our children feel defeated in areas such as school, sports, or relationships, we have a precious opportunity to teach them about the benefits of discipline and perseverance and to encourage them in the truth that God will give them the power to endure it. God never said life would be easy, but he did promise to never leave us or forsake us. "So we say with confidence, 'The Lord is my helper; I will not be afraid. What can mere mortals do to me?'" (Heb. 13:6). In him and through him, we have everything we will ever need.

> While we may not have control over what happens to us, we do have a say in how we respond and allow it to shape us as we turn to God in our need.

part 4

...

leading
with love
unconditional

chapter 18

authority
and obedience

*There is no fear in love. But perfect love
drives out fear, because fear has to do
with punishment. The one who fears
is not made perfect in love. We love
because he first loved us.*

—1 John 4:18–19

O ne of my favorite games to play with our children is "I love
you this much!" When we play this game, the first question I
ask them is, "How much do I love you?" In response they flash their
big beautiful smiles, stretch their arms out as wide as they can, and
shout, "This much!"

My next question in the game is always, "Does my love for you
ever change?" And again, they smile and boldly exclaim, "Nope, it
never changes," because they have come to learn that on their best
and worst days of behavior, my love for them is constant; it is unconditional. There is nothing they can do to make me love them any less

or any more, just as there is nothing they, or we, can do to diminish or increase God's love for and acceptance of us. In Christ, they are fully known, fully loved, *and* fully accepted.

When we allow this kind of unconditional love and acceptance to infuse our parenting, we reflect the heart of Jesus toward our children. This unconditional love of Jesus does not say, "Stop sinning, clean yourself up, then come to me and I will love you." No, Jesus, in his unconditional love, died for us *while* we were still sinners (Rom. 5:8). In Christ, we are simultaneously sinful in ourselves and righteous in Christ. Indeed we are ever in need of his grace: "For everyone has sinned; we all fall short of God's glorious standard. Yet God, with undeserved kindness, declares that we are righteous. He did this through Christ Jesus when he freed us from the penalty for our sins" (Rom. 3:23–24 NLT).

Jesus, in his unconditional love and undeserved kindness, is not in the business of fear, shame, rejection, or condemnation. Rather, he seeks to convict, redeem, and restore us through his grace — to set us free! This is how we know that Jesus loves us exactly as we are, but too much to leave us that way. This radical love of Jesus is not only unconditional but also transformative! And we will see in the following chapters how this love has the power to transform our children's hearts when we infuse it into the way we lead them.

In Control but Not Controlling

"How has God established his authority over my life?" That is the question we have to ask ourselves if our desire is to reflect God's heart in the way we establish authority with our children. See, God has given Mike and me authority over the children, but at the end of the day, we are all under God's authority. And what we know to be true is that God does not abuse or exploit his authority in our lives, nor would he honor our parenting our children in such a way.

In light of this knowledge, our desire should not be that our kids obey us out of fear and guilt, because fear and guilt do nothing to change the condition of the heart, and they don't reflect the heart of God. Now if you are thinking, "Hold on, Scripture tells us we should fear God—and God may use guilt to awaken us to our sin," you are right. Holy fear does lead to reverence for, awe of, and submission to God, and guilt that brings godly sorrow does lead us to repentance and obedience. Rather, I am referring to the fear and guilt that do not reflect the heart of God. Fear and guilt that tell us that God's love is conditional. Fear that tells us God is out to get us and that certain things are outside of God's ability to love and forgive. Guilt that brings shame, condemnation, and defeat and whispers, "You are unlovable and unworthy." Therefore, our purpose must be to teach our children about the sovereignty, the power, and the kindness of their heavenly Father's authority, and his desire to convict, redeem, and restore them through his amazing grace. Then we must pray for the Holy Spirit to pour through us and enable us to reflect God's heart in how we establish parental authority with our children.

> Our kids should not obey us out of fear and guilt, because fear and guilt do nothing to change the condition of the heart, and they don't reflect the heart of God.

To establish this kind of godly, grace-filled authority with our children, it's helpful to think about authority as being *in control* but not *controlling*. Tedd Tripp, in *Shepherding a Child's Heart*, wonderfully explains parental authority this way: "The purpose for your authority in the lives of your children is not to hold them under your power, but to empower them to be self-controlled people living freely under the authority of God."[20]

The authority that Tedd Tripp is describing here is not a fear-based, guilt-driven authority but one that is grounded in his perfect love. Over time, I have come to understand being in control as coming alongside my children rather than down on them. I'm learning how to allow God's grace to work through me to be an instrument of heart-changing grace in my children's lives. We want to use our authority to connect with our kids rather than to try to control them, because we are all, including our kids, designed for connection. Connection with God and connection with one another. To know and be known. To love and be loved. Connection draws us in; controlling authority makes us run.

> We want to use our authority to connect with our kids rather than to try to control them, because we are all designed for connection.

Our ability to establish godly, grace-filled authority with our children plays a key role in their obedience. This is why so much of our children's behavior contains the question, "Who is really in charge here—you or me?" Whether our kids realize it or not, they desperately need our answer to be "Mom and Dad are in charge," because children thrive within the boundaries of godly, grace-filled authority.

Testing Authority

I was reminded how important it is for our children to understand the constancy of our authority in their lives when I had to take Owen, who was eighteen months old at the time, to the radiology department of the hospital for X-rays of his chest. A tall man in a long white jacket escorted Owen and me down a long gray hallway and put us in a room that would easily seem spooky to an eighteen-month-old child. He proceeded to cover Owen and me in dark heavy jackets to protect certain parts of our bodies from being exposed to radiation. But the very second the technician took his hands off of Owen to walk over to the imaging machine to take the picture, Owen marched over to the far side of the room, jammed himself in the corner, and looked the technician right in the eye, as if to say "I dare you." Then, right on cue, the technician (who didn't exude a lot of confidence) said in his best sing-songy voice, "Come here, little guy—don't be afraid."

I wanted to tell the technician "A for effort" as Owen just stared back at him with a grin on his face that said, "Not happening, buddy." I'm pretty sure Owen was thinking, "Let's see who is really in charge here. Are you or am I? Because if you are not really in charge, I will not be getting up from this spot until you have left the building." Although the technician finally got the X-ray image he needed, it was no easy feat.

This situation was such a good reminder of how our children test our authority and try to make sense of it in their lives. Their words and actions beg the question, "Can I trust you to hold everything together?" And our honest answer is, "Well, actually, no, you can't. That is God's job. He is the one who holds everything together. You can, however, find security and assurance in the authority God has given me as your parent and in my commitment to uphold that authority out of my great love for you."

See, there is so much security and assurance for our children in knowing that Mom and Dad can be trusted to establish godly authority in their lives, not in a perfect or flawless way but in a way that says, "We say what we mean, and we mean what we say."

For example, Brennan often starts the day with what I simply call a test. He is ever in need of a reminder that he can trust in my authority as his mom, and in the boundaries we have set for him. So many of our mornings begin with Brennan ready for battle. But I know what he *really* is doing, in whatever battle he has chosen for that morning, is begging to be reminded that I will establish my authority with him and require him to exist within the boundaries of respect and kindness we have established in our home. Whether he realizes it or not, he wants to be reminded that I will exercise godly, grace-filled authority with him, an authority that is in control but not controlling. Our children want (and need) to know that they can trust in the authority they are submitting to. Just like I, at the end of the day, rely entirely on being able to trust in God's authority and sovereignty over my life.

> Say what you mean, and mean what you say.

This kind of godly, grace-filled authority says what it means and means what it says. It's an authority that seeks not to control but to empower kids in their response, as Tedd Tripp says, "to do what they do not want to do at the moment we ask them to do it."[21]

To empower our kids in their response to our authority, it usually is wise to offer them more than "Because I'm your mom and I said so," though at times this simple explanation is appropriate (especially after they have been lovingly taught the concepts of parental authority and child obedience). So let's focus on how to explain to our children the *whys* of obedience—both the motivation for and the benefits of obedience.

Why Obey? The Motivation for Obedience

In John 14:21, Jesus tells us, "Whoever has my commands and keeps them is the one who loves me. The one who loves me will be loved by my Father, and I too will love them and show myself to them." Jesus is making the link between love and obedience. Those who love him will desire to obey him. Love for Christ inspires obedience to Christ. But what fuels our love that inspires obedience? The answer is grace— the unconditional and wholehearted love of God in Christ Jesus.

This extravagant grace inspires our hearts to love, to trust, and to obey. I know this to be true in my own life, as it is the grace and love of God that fuels my desire to live in obedience to the will of God. I desire to honor and obey him because I trust in his unconditional love for me. I don't obey him to earn his acceptance, because his acceptance cannot be earned. I obey him because he already loves me. I obey him because he first loved me. In my sin, in my unworthiness, in my imperfection, he chose to love me with an everlasting love.

Once we embrace (as much as humanly possible) this unconditional love that he lavishes on us, our hearts are stirred to love, trust, and obey him.

In the same way, I am bold to suggest that our unconditional love for our children begets a willingness to submit to the authority that God has given us over them. Fear and guilt are not substantial motivators. They don't change the heart, and they don't bring transformation. Only the love of Jesus, infused into our parenting, does that.

> It is the grace and love of God that fuels my desire to live in obedience to the will of God.

It's the difference between guilt-driven obedience and grace-driven obedience. Guilt-driven obedience will be short-lived. It will be done with resentment, and it won't produce a heart that loves what Jesus loves. Grace-driven obedience, however, is motivated by a heart that has been captivated by Jesus' great love for them, and ours. It's obedience in response to a heart of love and gratitude.

Why Obey? The Benefits of Obedience

But what about the benefits of obedience? Do our children wonder, "Are there benefits to obeying Mommy and Daddy?" Or, to put it in their words, "What do I get out of it?"

If you'll recall, in chapter 10, we explored at length "the benefits"—the freedom and fullness of joy—that flow from obedience to our heavenly Father. We saw how his call to obedience is actually the blueprint to freedom from slavery to sin, guilt, and shame, how his way leads to an intimate relationship with him, and how his instructions for righteous living equip us for the purpose for which we were uniquely and wonderfully created.

This is the same wisdom I want to translate to the children when discussing the benefits of obeying us.

Therefore our message is, "Boys, we expect obedience because we love you. Our desire is to help you grow physically, mentally, emotionally, and spiritually. What we require of you is always intended for your good and God's glory, and it is always about helping you grow into the incredible man God created you to be. We want you to experience the freedom and abundant life that Jesus purchased for you through his death and resurrection." Or as Jesus put it, "If you keep my commands, you will remain in my love, just as I have kept my Father's commands and remain in his love. I have told you this so that my joy may be in you and that your joy may be complete" (John 15:10–11).

The *How* of Obedience

In addition to exploring the crucial *why* of obedience, we also need to focus on the *how* of obedience. The three main areas of *how* include:

1. How much obedience should we expect?
2. How quickly should we expect obedience?
3. How do we expect their obedience to be wrapped?

How Much Obedience Should We Expect?

To know how much obedience to expect, we can start by looking at the words of Jesus. What does he say about obedience? "If you love me, obey my commandments" (John 14:15 NLT). Obedience is evidence of love, the fruit of a life attached to "the vine." That being said, let us not pretend that we, or our children, are capable of perfect obedience. We are all sinners, desperately in need of the grace of our Savior. This is why it is so important that we are able and willing to say to our kids, "I know why you don't obey all the time. I get it. Mommy doesn't obey perfectly either! Thank God for Jesus who obeyed perfectly on our behalf."

With this truth in mind, we must start by recognizing that our children cannot, and will not, have perfect obedience (which is something I actually once expected of my children because I was foolishly expecting it of myself). But as parents responsible for instructing our children in the truth, we still must require obedience, teach our children about the consequences of sin and disobedience (which is dramatically different from condemnation for disobedience), and encourage them to rely on the inexhaustible power of the Holy Spirit to live in obedience.

How Quickly Should We Expect Obedience?

So how quickly should we expect obedience? How quickly do we expect our children to do what they do not want to do at the moment we want them to do it? Well, let's start by considering the burning issue in so many parenting books: to count or not to count. When we require obedience from our children, should we count to three, should we count to five, should we count forward, or should we count backward?

Rather than answer that specific question, I want to offer you a few thoughts to ponder that have been useful for us in determining the standard for our family:

- Do you expect your child to obey the first time you ask, or are you open to asking multiple times before they obey?
- Do you feel your child should get one, two, three seconds to

ponder the question, "Mom just asked me to do something I don't want to do, but I'm doing something I really want to do, so now what am I going to do?"

- Do you believe that "delayed obedience is disobedience" and therefore anything other than an immediate response is disobedience?

These are not easy questions to answer, but as I pondered these questions myself and reflected on our purpose in requiring obedience, I ended up creating what I call the "R & R principle." The R & R stands for *respectful* and *reasonable*, meaning our children need to be respectful, and we need to be reasonable.

A respectful response from our children requires a "say and do."

For example, when I ask Brennan to come to the table, he has two choices that I will accept as respectful. First option: Say, "Yes, Mommy," and do as I've asked and come to the table. Second option: Say, "Yes, Mommy," and ask a question in a respectful way. An example would be, "But may I first finish putting together the Lego tower I'm building?"

Through these two options you can see how a respectful response essentially means "Yes, Mommy, with obedience" or "Yes, Mommy, and may I?"

A reasonable response from us often requires us to stop and assess the situation rather than offering, "Just obey me now." In aiming to be reasonable, there are times when I will respond with, "Thank you for asking respectfully; yes, you may finish your tower," and there are other times that I will respond with, "No, not today, honey. I need you to come to the table now, but thank you for asking respectfully." Our reasonable response affirms their respectful request.

How Do We Expect Their Obedience to Be Wrapped?

With what attitude do we expect our children's obedience to be wrapped? My son Owen struggles at times to wrap his obedience in willingness. He typically oozes love, but when he doesn't get his way or he is asked to do something he doesn't want to do, his angelic little face sometimes transforms into what I call "cranky face." In our home, obeying with "cranky face" is not much better than flat-out disobeying. It's a step; it's definitely a step. He has made the choice to obey, and I don't negate that. However, the goal is to obey without grumbling or complaining.

Should we always expect our kids to make their beds with gladness, take their dishes to the sink with laughter, or clean up their toys with cheer? Of course not. But should we tolerate complaining and whining because they have responsibilities? Not a chance. Therefore when I say the goal is obeying without grumbling or complaining, I mean it's about obedience becoming something our kids do willingly, perhaps even gladly, recognizing that obeying Mom and Dad is one of the ways they can glorify God: "Children, obey your parents in everything, for this pleases the Lord" (Col. 3:20).

Establishing authority and requiring obedience in this way is an approach that is at once firm and gentle, reflecting the loving heart of Jesus for our kids.

chapter 19

training and instruction

And this is his command: to believe in the name of his Son, Jesus Christ, and to love one another as he commanded us. The one who keeps God's commands lives in him, and he in them. And this is how we know that he lives in us: We know it by the Spirit he gave us.

—1 John 3:23–24

When we do nothing, we still do something. Think about it. If we ignore disrespect, we teach our children that rudeness is acceptable. If we ignore a lie, we teach them that dishonesty is tolerable, or perhaps even has its rewards. And if we allow our kids to say awful things to each other, we teach them that self-control is superfluous and anger can wage its war in our home. This is why we must be intentional and purposeful in the way we train our children.

If common Christian parenting practices tell us anything, it's this: we stop reading Ephesians 6 after the first two sentences and we fail to realize that this passage, in its entirety, offers instructions for children and parents alike. "Children, obey your parents in the Lord, for this is right. 'Honor your father and mother'—which is the first commandment with a promise—'so that it may go well with you and that you may enjoy long life on the earth.' Fathers, do not exasperate your children; instead, bring them up in the training and instruction of the Lord" (Eph. 6:1–4).

We are prone to focus only on the command to children to obey their parents, and we miss out on one of the only two verses in the New Testament that is actually written as a direct command to parents in childrearing: to instruct and train their children in the grace and truth of Jesus Christ.

● ● ● ● ● ● ● ● ● ● ● ● ● ● ● ●

When we do nothing, we still do something.

● ● ● ● ● ● ● ● ● ● ● ● ● ● ● ●

Elyse Fitzpatrick and Jessica Thompson, in their incredible book *Give Them Grace*, offer extraordinary understanding of this verse and its relation to the role parents play in instructing and training their children. They write, "Paul's command to 'bring them up in the discipline and instruction of the Lord' means this: that parents are to think about and remember Jesus Christ and then train their children to understand how everything in their life—their joys and sorrows, their trials and labors, their doubts, sin and shame—is to be understood and approached in the light of Jesus Christ.... That is the best news any child could hear."[22]

Now before we move on to explore this command further, I want to point out another common but often misunderstood verse as it relates to Christian parenting, which is Proverbs 22:6: "Start children off on the way they should go, and even when they are old they will not turn from it." Here we should note that we find not a promise or a command for parents but rather a proverb, a piece of wisdom. Let us remember that the Proverbs are not if–then promises. They were "written to instill skill in the art of godly living in those who heed their counsel."[23] Therefore, what Proverbs 22:6 does offer is wise counsel, encouraging parents to identify and develop the unique personality, disposition, and giftedness that God has hidden in their child to his glory. We can't, however, interpret this proverb as a promise to parents that they will have children with vibrant faith.

What we can assuredly conclude through the direct command we find in Ephesians 6, and the piece of wisdom we find in Proverbs 22, is this: Our training should be focused on teaching our children that everything in life is to be approached through the grace and truth of Jesus Christ. And we are wise to seek out what God has hidden in our children and develop those gifts to the glory of God and not self.

We can also assuredly conclude that neither of these things will happen by accident. As we discussed in chapter 2, parents have to be intentional in discipling their children, because even when we don't intentionally train our children, we can rest assured that we are indeed still training them. Though we may not be training what we'd hoped. Just as physical training is essential to a sport, so is godly training essential to raising our children in the way they should go. For example, an athlete trains his body so that it's conditioned to do exactly what he wants it to do at the moment he wants it done. Therefore, my husband, an avid golfer, must train himself to focus on his grip, stance, and ball position while keeping his head still and swinging with perfect tempo if he wants to play to his best potential. Golfing requires physical instruction and

> Our training should be focused on teaching our children that everything in life is to be approached through the grace and truth of Jesus Christ.

training, just as being intentional and purposeful in raising our kids in the truth and grace of Jesus Christ requires godly instruction and training. Paul was the first to draw this helpful analogy between physical and godly training: "Train yourself to be godly. For physical training is of some value, but godliness has value for all things, holding promise for both the present life and the life to come. This is a trustworthy saying that deserves full acceptance" (1 Tim. 4:7–9).

You Choose

Rather than ignore our children's behavior, we ought to seize the valuable opportunity to train them to rely on God to empower them to make choices that honor him. This is what I call "You Choose!"

When I see our children struggling with an attitude or a behavior, I tell them that they have an important choice to make and the outcome will be based solely on what they choose to do. For example, if the boys are being unkind to each other, I ask, "Are you being kind to each other?" Of course, they answer no, and in response I say, "Well, you have some important choices to make. You can choose to make a good choice—to be kind—and in turn anticipate a good outcome, or you can choose to make a poor choice—continue to fight—and expect a consequence. You choose."

I will often remind my children of Philippians 2:13 (NLT), "For God is working in you, giving you the desire and the power to do what pleases him." This verse reminds them that God can give them the *desire* and the *power* to honor him in what they choose, and it teaches them that while they may not have it in them to be kind to one another, Christ *in them* does. Or as 1 John 4:4 (NLT) puts it, "But you belong to God, my dear children. You have already won a victory.... because the Spirit who lives in you is greater than the spirit who lives in the world."

A great example of this type of scenario recently played out on our kitchen floor. Brennan began the day with one of his "tests." I could tell he woke up ready for battle as I listened to his little feet stomp across the hardwood floor from his bedroom to the kitchen. When he arrived in the kitchen, he began complaining about the fact that Daddy did not kiss him good-bye and he didn't like the break-fast I'd prepared. When Brennan was finished with his laundry list of complaints, I said, "My sweet Brennan, I love you, and I will not allow you to disrupt our morning with your lack of self-control and unthankful spirit. I need you to return to the privacy of your own room, ask Jesus to help you find your self-control, think about what you can be thankful for, and then you may join the rest of the family in the kitchen."

> What started out as a very bad, no-good day turned into a precious opportunity to train him and encourage him to rely on Jesus as his source of strength.

I listened to Brennan stomp back to his room, but after about only five seconds, I heard the stomping again. He was on his way back to dish out another round of whatever you want to call it. As he came around the corner, he threw himself on the floor and loudly declared, "I can't find it! I cannot find my self-control anywhere! It's gone!"

While trying to squelch the laughter that was dying to burst forth, I joined Brennan on the floor, held him close, and gently asked, "Honey, did you take the time to ask Jesus to give you the desire, and the power, to show self-control?"

I already knew the answer, but I waited for Brennan to exhale, "No, Mom. I didn't." And together, we bowed our heads and prayed that Jesus would live his life through Brennan and help him have self-control and a thankful spirit.

The point is what started out as a very bad, no-good day turned into a precious opportunity to train him and encourage him to rely on Jesus as his source of strength. That is what "You Choose" is all about—being purposeful in training our children in the truth and grace of Jesus. It's essentially godly training.

The Power of (God's) Words

When we picked Cal up from school, Brennan proudly informed him that while he was at the pool earlier in the day, he finally had the courage to take off his floaties and swim from the shallow end to the deep end of the pool without help. Unfortunately, when Brennan was done with his story, Cal looked at him and murmured, "Oh, man, that's so easy." The look on Brennan's face was one of complete defeat. I'm pretty sure he'd been waiting all day to tell his big brother this exciting news, all the while hoping his big brother would say something like, "Awesome job, Brennan!" But no such luck.

I turned to Cal and explained, "You know, baby, your words have power."

He gave me a perplexed look, like he often does when I use obscure expressions, and asked, "What do you mean, Mom?"

I reminded Cal of Proverbs 18:21 (NKJV): "Death and life are in the power of the tongue, and those who love it will eat its fruit."

I explained how this verse teaches us that our words can typically do one of two things. They can build up, or they can tear down. They can bring life, or they can bring death. And I explained that although he may not have meant to hurt his brother's feelings, his words were indeed hurtful. We then talked about the other things he could have said to build his little brother up and congratulate him for overcoming his fear of swimming without help.

Our kids' words are not the only words that have power. As parents, the words that we use to instruct and train our children also hold power. This is why, in times of instruction and training, we should rely on the words the apostle Paul uses to describe the fruit of the Spirit: love, joy, peace, patience, kindness, goodness, faithfulness, gentleness, and self-control (Gal. 5:22–23). In referring to these nine virtues of the Christian life, we can be specific about what we hope to see as the overflow of their heart.

For instance, if Cal is playing too rough with his little brother and we ask, "Cal, are you being a good boy?" he will probably respond with, "No, Mom, I'm not." But what exactly is *good*, and what are we really trying to teach him in that moment? Therefore, rather than using a generic word like *good*, my question may sound something more like, "Cal, are you being gentle or kind to your brother?"

Or if Brennan is tattling on his brother for watching a show he isn't allowed to watch I can ask, "Brennan, are you being a peacemaker? Did you first encourage Cal to make a good choice or are you just trying to get him in trouble?"

Using specific words for the virtues we desire to instill in our kids is one simple and easy way we can point them back to Christ and the fruit of the Spirit. Remember, if words are powerful (and they are), God's Words are supreme, for "all Scripture is God-breathed and is useful for teaching, rebuking, correcting and training in righteousness" (2 Tim. 3:16).

> Using specific words for the virtues we desire to instill in our kids is one simple and easy way we can point them back to Christ and the fruit of the Spirit.

Ask, Don't Tell

Another simple but profound way we can instruct and train our children is by using what I call the "ask, don't tell" policy in parenting.

It's really quite simple, but oh so profound, and it merely entails asking our kids questions rather than telling them what we have observed.

Asking questions is key, as questions are so much more effective than statements when we are trying to reach our children's hearts. For instance, if we simply tell our children what we expect of them, our statement is likely to go in one ear and out the other. However, if we ask a question, our kids are required to identify their behavior and reflect on the effect their actions have on others.

For example, if I see the boys struggling to share a toy, I have one of two choices in how I can proceed to instruct and train them.

My first option is to say to them, "Kids, you aren't sharing. All of this arguing is not acceptable, and you need to be peacemakers."

My second option is to say to them, "Kids, are you fighting over that toy? Can you tell Mommy what a peacemaker would do? What does it mean to treat others the way that we want to be treated?"

While option one is a batch of true but jumbled observations, option two (which reflects the "ask, don't tell" principle) involves training our children to think through the scenario, assess their actions, and grow in their empathy and problem-solving skills.

Stop plus Start

"Stop plus start" is another key training tool, and it speaks to the importance of focusing on what you want to train your children to start doing rather than on what you want them to stop doing. Looking back at my days as a first-time mom, in the throes of containing (as best I knew how) an eighteen-month-old, I can see how so much of my instruction lacked specificity. As I watched Cal begin to explore his surroundings, most of my sentences began and ended with a bold "no!" The problem was "No climbing the stairs without Mommy!" and "No eating dog food!" were rarely followed up with what I actually wanted him to do. I was more focused on getting him to stop, rather than start, a particular behavior.

For example, Owen, our third son, who is now four, had a particular fascination with all things electronic. And like most, if not all, toddlers, he loved the remote control. If he picked up the remote and I said, "Owen, no. Do not touch the remote control," I have taught him only what not to do. Instructing and training requires that I follow up my no with, "Now please put it down and walk away. Let's find a fun toy to play with." Of course he didn't understand this instruction the first time I said it, but over time, "No plus walk away and find something else to do" came to "equal" something to him.

This idea of stop plus start is just as applicable to my eight-year-old and five-year-old as it is to my four-year-old, as long as I include choices for our older boys to make in the process. My dear friend Heather actually calls it "rewind and retry." When Cal speaks to me in an unacceptable way, I begin with, "Cal, is it respectful to speak to me that way?" When he answers, "No, Mom, it's not," I follow up with, "You must speak to me with respect. Please choose words and a tone that I can listen to." Or when Brennan gets angry with Cal and lashes out at him, I begin with, "Brennan, is it kind to hit your brother?" When he replies, "No, it's not, Mom," I follow up with, "Do you think that using your words instead of your hands could have been a better choice? Can you show Mommy how you show self-control with your actions?"

I know they are learning, because I have begun to hear them speak to each other in the same way I instruct them. In fact, while the boys were recently playing together in their room, I heard a sharp scream, followed by Brennan loudly declaring, "Cal, stop pushing me! You are supposed to use your words, not your hands!" Without realizing it, Brennan gave a stop plus start directive to his brother.

Taking "Do-Overs" for Granted

In training our children with the stop plus start approach, we have to be careful that we do not get stuck in this pattern: misbehavior plus correction and training equals good behavior. I recently got stuck in this rut, and it got to the point that the children were rarely ever listening the first time, because they knew Mommy would give them a stop plus start directive before implementing consequences. They were taking their "do-overs" for granted, but after a full day of "no second chances," we were back on track.

For instance, when Brennan dropped his backpack in the back seat of the car and immediately shouted, "*Mom*, I dropped my backpack! Get it now!" I replied, "No, Brennan, I will not. And I will not give you a second chance. Mommy will not be spoken to that way. Unfortunately you have gotten into the habit of speaking disrespectfully to me, even yelling at me at times, and then requiring correction to speak kindly. When we arrive at home, you can unbuckle and get it yourself, but I will not be helping you. In the meantime you can sit there and think about why you spoke to Mommy that way, and I will listen when you are ready to apologize."

Sure enough, the next afternoon when he dropped his stuffed tiger in the back seat of the car, he kindly said, "Mom, will you please get my tiger off the floor? I just dropped it." I praised him for speaking with respect and grabbed his tiger at the first red light.

> There is such a thing as "over-training" our children.

Simultaneously I did the same type of training with Cal. As we were leaving the pool, he begged to go home with his cousins. He proceeded to complain and argue until I finally said, "You know, I was going to allow you to go home with them, but because you have argued and complained while I tried to figure out the details, I now have to say no. Tomorrow, if you can ask with respect, and wait patiently for me to decide, the answer will most likely be yes. But today, the answer is no." And sure enough, the next day at the pool, he so much remembered the lesson that he said, "Mom, I am asking you kindly if I can go home with my cousins. Is that okay?" I was so thrilled to be able to reply, "Of course you can, and I am so proud of you for learning the lesson."

And while this type of training and instruction is critical for our children, let me say I do believe that there is also such a thing as "over-training" our children.

Over-training

During a recent visit to Birmingham to visit my oldest sister, Patti, who has three children many years older than mine, she noticed how much training and correcting I was doing with the boys. This was partially because my kids were in a house with no age-appropriate toys, their cousins were all involved in summer activities, and I was more focused on catching up with my sister than I was on proactively parenting my kids. It didn't take long for things to unravel. After two full days of hearing me train and instruct my children every time they misbehaved, my sister said, "Jeannie, you know, sometimes it's okay to just say no, or stop and move on." And she was right. I was overtraining my children when, at this point, they should have been fully aware of the reasons we expect certain behaviors from them. I have to remind myself that it is okay to occasionally just say no, because when I talk *all* the time, they stop listening. Eventually, it all begins to sound the same.

Another problem was that because of the amount of instructing and training I was doing, I began to keep my eyes open only for what they were doing wrong. You see, too often we see only what we are looking for. So if we're only on "sin patrol," looking for the ways in which our children need to be corrected or disciplined, we miss the beautiful moments when we can encourage them in the virtues that *are* flowing from their hearts. Which leads us to my next point—the invaluable role of encouragement in instruction and training.

Specific and Sincere Praise

Take a moment and ask yourself, "What would it look like if I spent more time looking at my children the way Jesus looks at me?" What if I spent more time thinking about how I can encourage my kids in God's grace instead of focusing on the times when they sin or misbehave? This all goes back to your image of Jesus. If you think of Jesus as someone who is waiting to catch you in your sin, you may be inclined to parent that way. But if you understand him to be a God who seeks to convict rather than condemn, a God who is desiring to redeem and restore rather than shame and guilt, a God who isn't waiting to catch you in your sin but is delighting in your willingness to surrender to his grace, you may be more inclined to parent your children that way as well.

> Take a moment and ask yourself, "What would it look like if I spent more time looking at my children the way Jesus looks at me?"

Using specific and sincere praise when instructing and training our children is a wonderful way to reflect the heart of Jesus for our kids. I call this "S & S praise."

When we are specific with our encouragement and praise, we let our children know exactly what it is that prompts us to praise them. In praising our kids, we always want to be looking for opportunities to praise them for relying on God to give them the desire and the strength to honor him. Of course this kind of praise is not always realistic or possible. Still, it's great to remember that praise that points our kids back to God's grace at work in their lives and praise that recognizes the fruit of the Spirit flowing from their hearts are the best forms of encouragement we can give them.

Sincerity is also crucial when we encourage and praise our children. For example, if my husband told me that I sounded like Carrie Underwood when I sing my heart out, I would know that he, unfortunately, wasn't being sincere. I wish it were true, but the truth is my singing voice is not what I thought it was when I was given most of the solos at church as a young child. (I have since learned that, *of course*, the preacher's kid gets the solos.)

Now let's apply this concept of specificity to one of our boys. Cal, for example, is a great athlete, but he is also ultra-competitive. He plays his heart out, and he does not like to lose, especially when he feels like a mistake he made in the game hurt the outcome. Therefore, even if he didn't personally have his best game, I can offer him specific and sincere praise that he gave 100 percent and he didn't quit. I can praise his passion and his effort. There is usually *something* we can specifically and sincerely praise.

In looking at why both specificity and sincerity are important in praise, we can return to our value of honesty: our children need to know that we speak the truth. And we return to the idea of the power of specific words, the idea that targeted, rather than generic, words hold more power and meaning. For example, here are some generic words of praise parents tend to offer, contrasted to specific and sincere things we might say to encourage and praise our children:

Generic: "Owen, you are such a good boy!"

S & S: "Owen, I just caught you showing self-control when your brother took a toy from you! You used your words instead of your hands. Great job!"

Generic: "Cal, you are so smart. You do really well in school."

S & S: "Cal, I really like the way you focused on completing your homework. I know you are working really hard on improving your concentration, and I'm proud of you!"

Generic: "Brennan, you are a great big brother!"

S & S: "Brennan, I love the way you just built your little brother up. You have such a loving heart, and it brings Mommy so much joy when I see you encouraging your brother!"

One of the many, but often overlooked, benefits of this kind of sincere and specific praise is that it tends to motivate children who have not made praiseworthy choices. My praise for the obedient child ends up motivating another child who is choosing not to obey.

For example, in a concerted effort to get out the door quickly, I told Cal and Brennan I needed them to go to the front door and put on their shoes and jackets. Two minutes later I arrived at the door to find Brennan doing exactly what I'd asked of him—sitting on the floor, jacket on, just finishing up tying his shoes. Cal, on the other hand, was still sitting on the floor reading his book, no shoes or jacket in sight. I will admit my first instinct was to growl, "Cal, why are you still sitting there? Why are you not ready?" (And indeed, that is sometimes exactly what I do.) But, in this instance, I chose praise.

I happily exclaimed, "Brennan, I am so proud of you for doing exactly what I asked you to do the first time. You obeyed Mommy and that was great listening, pal." At that precise moment, Cal's ears perked up and he sprang into action, because he wanted a little piece of the praise too. I didn't say, "Cal, I can't believe you didn't do as I asked. Brennan, good job, you did a much better job than Cal listening." I didn't compare them with each other; I simply praised the one who obeyed. I was intentional and purposeful in building Brennan up, and this inspired Cal to obey.

Now of course, this isn't the *reason* we should praise our kids when they make good choices; it just happens to be a by-product of it. You see, we do have to be careful with this kind of motivation, because while it is a wonderful thing to inspire obedience in our kids through sincere and specific praise, we must also make sure that praise, or rewards, do not become our child's primary motivation for obedience.

Rewards-Based Instruction

Therefore, before we close this chapter, it's important we acknowledge the significant role that rewards-based instruction and training plays in our society. Rewards-based training essentially gives your children positive goals to work toward rather than just negative consequences to avoid, and rewards are given *after* the desired behavior has occurred.

Giving our children rewards is not necessarily a bad thing, but because rewards-based parenting used to be my way of trying to control my kids' behavior, I now know how ineffective it is, at least in the long term, and how little it reaches their hearts. We had sticker charts for all to see who was getting ahead and who was falling behind. And we had jelly bean jars so they could put jelly beans into the jar when they did well and they could take jelly beans out of the jar when they failed to do well. You name it, I probably tried it — charts and jars and various other schemes to control my kids to get them to do exactly what I wanted them to do.

> You name it, I probably tried it — charts and jars and various other schemes to control my kids to get them to do exactly what I wanted them to do.

Now please hear this: I am not judging your jelly bean jar or sticker chart (if you happen to have one). I am only confessing the ways in which my charts and jars were stealing our joy and giving our kids more "law" than their sweet souls could bear. I am only taking my own inventory here, because I can speak only about the motivation of my own heart. Motivation—that's the key. My motivation in using charts and jelly bean jars was to control my kids. Control. Such a life-sucking force. It wasn't until I realized that Jesus doesn't have a jelly bean jar that I was able to surrender mine.

You can see then how we must be careful that rewards do not become the motivation for our children's behavior. Earlier we looked at what Scripture says should motivate obedience, and it is certainly not rewards; rather it is love for God. However I do, as a parent, very much enjoy giving my children rewards (and the rewards are not just material things). I love seeing the joy on their faces when they receive a reward, just as I believe our heavenly Father enjoys giving good gifts to us and takes pleasure in our enjoying those gifts.

I don't dare equate my giving rewards to my children for good behavior with the way that our heavenly Father gives good gifts to us. We never want to suggest to our children that the riches of his grace flow only when we obey. This is not the case at all, and it certainly isn't the message of unconditional love. I simply enjoy pointing out the fact that just as I enjoy blessing and rewarding our kids, so too does our heavenly Father, and in much greater extravagance. "If you, then, though you are evil, know how to give good gifts to your children, how much more will your Father in heaven give good gifts to those who ask him!" (Matt. 7:11).

As long as they don't come to expect tangible rewards for the wise choices they make, I think we are on track. And if a question comes (which it certainly has), such as, "What is my reward for letting my brother go first?" then I know we have to refocus our rewards on what I call a verbal high-five, which is essentially, "I am really proud of you for making such a good choice. I see you being so kind to your brothers today, and I know Jesus delights in your kindness."

The goal is to keep their heart and mind focused on doing the right thing—for the right reason.

Instructing and training our children in this way helps us develop their gifts to the glory of God and not self, and it demonstrates how everything in life is to be understood through the grace and truth of Jesus Christ.

chapter 20

discipline
and correction

No discipline seems pleasant at the time,
but painful. Later on, however, it produces
a harvest of righteousness and peace
for those who have been trained by it.

—Hebrews 12:11

Brennan is a child who gets particularly excited about his birthday. There is just something about getting a little bit older that Brennan really likes. I assume he thinks he's catching up to his big brother without realizing that Cal is also getting older! Nonetheless, when Brennan turned four, we threw a party for him that ended up being called the "Brennan Birthday Bonanza." He was in all his glory. After the cake was eaten and his little buddies left our home, we let Brennan open all of his presents. One by one, he opened the gifts but refused to let his brothers play with them, much less touch them. After I gave him several reminders that he would need to let his brothers look at his new toys or we would have to take a break from opening gifts, I had to send him to his room.

I explained, "Brennan, I know you are so excited, and I know this is a really special day. I have been patient with your unwillingness to share your new toys, but I will not give you any more warnings. I need you to go to your room and think about what's going on in your heart and why you won't allow your brothers to see what you have been given."

A few minutes later, I joined Brennan in his room and I noticed that he was more upset than usual. I sat down on the edge of his bed, and I asked him what was going on his heart. With tears running down his face he said, "You love Cal and Owen more than me. You sent me to my room on my birthday, and they are still playing with my new toys, so you love them more than you love me."

Ouch! I sat there dumbfounded for a moment wondering, "What have I done to send him that message? How can I help him understand that it is because of my great love for him that I discipline him?"

I gathered my thoughts and attempted to share this message: "Brennan, I love each one of you completely and totally. You are each so special, wonderfully and uniquely created in the image of your heavenly Father. My heart grew with love each time God gave us another child. I don't love your brothers any more or any less than I love you. I love you each like crazy. And because I love you this much, I discipline you, so that you can continue to grow into the incredible boy that God created you to be."

Well, my explanation made as much sense as it can to a four-year-old (which evidently isn't much), because he then asked, "Do you love Henry that much too?" (You should know, Henry is our dog.) I assured Brennan that I love Henry very much and I think he is a super dog, but I explained that I don't love Henry with the same depth that I love him and his brothers. Evidently this was another inadequate answer, because he responded by sobbing, "Well, that isn't very nice, Mommy! You should love Henry like you love us!"

So essentially, Brennan had gone from being sad about feeling like he was loved less than his brothers, to being sad that he was actually loved more than his dog. And the point is it's impossible for our kids to fully comprehend our love for them, and it can be exponentially harder for them to understand how our love for them has anything to do with our discipline.

Loving our children through discipline is not a fun job. We might avoid discipline out of guilt, exhaustion, or even fear. But just as the Lord trains and disciplines those he loves, we must also do the same for our children, as Proverbs 3:11–12 says, "My son, do not despise the LORD's discipline, and do not resent his rebuke, because the LORD disciplines those he loves, as a father the son he delights in."

> Just as the Lord trains and disciplines those he loves, we must also do the same for our children.

Discipline versus Punishment

When God disciplines us he is not trying to show us who's boss. He desires to lovingly rescue us. Why would we do any differently with our kids?

Helping our children understand the role of discipline in our lives—and how discipline differs from punishment—is crucial. James Dobson, in his book *Dare to Discipline*, makes an important distinction between punishment and discipline. He explains that punishment is directed at the person, while discipline is directed at the behavior.[24] This is not only a really important concept for us to translate to our children but it's also a wonderful opportunity to remind our children of the good news of our Savior.

You see, Jesus already bore the punishment for our sins through his finished work on the cross. And because of his extravagant sacrifice, we do not have to endure the punishment for our sins—we do not have to pay the ultimate price for our sins—because the price has been paid in full. The Lord does, however, grow us with corrective discipline. And, likewise, we are instructed to grow our children with corrective discipline.

> When God disciplines us he is not trying to show us who's boss. He desires to lovingly rescue us. Why would we do any differently with our kids?

To reflect the heart of Jesus to our kids, our approach with our children can never be, "Shame on you for disobeying me. I will now punish you because you are bad." Let me say that again, our purpose should never be to shame our children by using words such as "You are a bad boy" or "You are a bad girl," because statements such as "You are a bad boy" and "You are a bad girl" are directed at the personhood of our children, rather than at the behavior they have displayed. Punishment, directed at the personhood of our children, is shame inducing, and it will never reach our children's hearts. Shame believes the lie that because I do unlovable things, I am therefore an unlovable person. But Jesus never confused the two. Jesus does not shame us, nor should we shame our children. Rather, we want to grow our children with corrective discipline—discipline that reflects God's holy discipline in our lives.

What Is Sin?

An important piece to discipline is helping our children understand what sin is and how it grieves the heart of God. See, too often people think of sin as merely the things we do that we shouldn't have done or the things we should have done but didn't. But the truth is that *sinful* is the very state in which we exist; it is our fallen nature. And because of our fallen nature we make choices that are not in line with who God created us to be. Even in our finest moments, our actions, if not our motives, are tainted (Gen. 6:5).

Sin can be explained in several ways, but a few ways that resonate with our children include breaking God's law, choosing my way over God's way, and making something or someone more important than God.

When we teach our children what sin is, it is equally important that we teach them what sin does to our hearts, minds, bodies, and souls, and the inevitable pain and disappointment that result from our sin. We must teach our children that God hates sin, that it grieves God's heart, and that our sin is what nailed Jesus to the cross. And then, yes then, we must offer our children the very good and beautiful news that when they confess their sin, they are unconditionally forgiven, accepted, and loved.

I know that many parents cringe at the idea of talking to their kids about sin. Something about it just doesn't sit right with us. On so many occasions, I have had conversations with parents who ask, "How can I tell my five-year-old that she is a sinner? It doesn't feel good." One mom explained, "When I tell my son he's a sinner, it feels like I'm telling my child

> Revelation of our sin leads us to revel in God's grace.

that God is mad at him." I can see why talking about sin would seem awful if we think that "God is mad at you" is the message we are sending, but the message is actually just the opposite. It's good news, and here is why: If we don't see ourselves as sinners, then we don't see our need for a Savior. And we have a Savior who loves sinners. Revelation of our sin leads us to revel in God's grace.

Let us not forget that kids have an innate understanding, a God-given conscience, when something is wrong. And speaking to our kids about their sin is actually an opportunity to give them hope. Yes, hope! Our sin points us to our only hope—the rescuer we've been given in Jesus Christ, who frees us from our slavery to sin (Rom. 6:17–18) and frees us to love with the love we've first been given.

So when we teach our kids how to recognize and confess sin in their life, we must finish with a drenching of grace. Sin is *what we do* in our fallen nature. Wholeheartedly loved and accepted children of God is *who we are* in Jesus Christ. We can't out-sin his love! Do you see how the story does not end with "you are a sinner"? It ends with "you have a Savior." Thank God for Jesus. In his grace we are forgiven, and there is nothing that can separate us from the love of God that is in Christ Jesus our Lord (Rom. 8:39).

> There is nothing that can separate us from the love of God that is in Christ Jesus our Lord. Absolutely nothing.

Absolutely nothing. Loving our children this way is how we reflect the Father's heart for them.

Now let's see how a conversation about sin (one that distinguishes between punishment and discipline) can play out with our kids.

It was Cal's Saturday to have a date with Daddy, but unfortunately he had spent the last several days consistently testing the boundaries of authority and respect in our home. Honestly, it was one of those weeks that make me completely question my ability to raise children. So when Saturday morning arrived and we had to tell Cal that he was not going to have a special outing in New York City with his dad on this particular day, we knew it was going to devastate him.

Cal had been so looking forward to his special day, as was his dad. And it hurt us both to see Cal so sad. But we knew that this situation required discipline. Sure, Cal and Daddy still spent time alone together that day, but it was time spent talking about what was going on in Cal's heart and helping Cal understand why he made the choices he had made. It was not a "bad dog" conversation. Mike did not shame or guilt Cal for the way he behaved; instead he told Cal how much it grieved him that they could not keep their special plans for the day. He talked to him about how disrespect and unthankfulness are not what we, or God, desire for Cal. He talked to Cal about not only his sin but also his Savior, who forgives his sin. And Mike made sure Cal knew that the discipline was rooted in our unconditional love for him and our desire to see him grow into the incredible man God created him to be.

Consistency versus Empty Threats

It goes without saying, but I will say it anyway: children thrive within consistent and enforced boundaries and discipline.

For your children to trust that you mean what you say, your expectations must be enforced consistently. Empty threats are completely self-defeating, not to mention exhausting. I shudder to think of some of the ridiculous threats I have made, knowing full well there was no way I could, or would, follow through. There was always that little voice in my head saying, "I really hope they don't call my bluff."

I recently witnessed the following "empty threat" scenario play out between a mother and daughter in the grocery store. A little girl spotted a piece of candy that she really, *really* wanted in the checkout line. The mom told her daughter that she could not have the candy, but the little girl persisted. Her persistence quickly turned to wailing, and then she ran for the front door of the grocery store with the candy in her hand. Now we've all been the victim of the grocery store meltdown, so I promise I am not judging this worn-out mom who shouted out to her fleeing daughter, "If you leave this store, the policeman outside the door will scoop you up and take you to jail. You better come back here!"

Yes, her daughter did return to her, but the core problem remained. The empty threat may have saved the mom in the heat of the moment when her three-year-old decided that she didn't want to go to jail, but it did nothing for the condition of her daughter's heart and the battle she will certainly, and I mean certainly, wage again.

Inconsistent discipline essentially teaches our children to challenge us. It teaches them that arguing, begging, and throwing a full-blown fit will change our mind and give them the outcome they desire—at any cost to our sanity. We don't do them, or ourselves, any favors by being inconsistent.

One of the ways I reinforce my commitment to consistency with our kids is by asking them this simple question when they argue or beg: "Please tell Mommy of a time when begging or arguing has worked in your favor?"

> Inconsistent discipline essentially teaches our children to challenge us.

For example, if Cal begs for something in the checkout line after I have clearly said no to his request, I will look in his eyes and ask, "Cal, please tell Mommy of a time when begging or arguing has worked in your favor." And at that request, Cal will huff, "Never," because he knows with complete certainty that arguing and begging do not achieve his desired outcome.

Rather than call me consistent, you could call me uptight, rigid, and unwilling to compromise, but please hear me out. Of course we must listen to our child's feelings and allow them to respectfully explain their desire or their reason for a request. And there are certainly times when we should remain open to allowing their reasoning (when done in a respectful way) to influence our decisions, but it should never be as a result of their arguing and begging. This goes back to the R & R principle. They must be respectful, and we must be reasonable.

For example, if Cal is reading a book, and I say, "Cal, it's time to stop reading and come to the table," a few different scenarios can play out:

1. Cal can say, "Yes, Mommy," and head on over.
2. Cal can ignore me (pretend he didn't hear me) and keep on reading.
3. Cal can argue with a rude tone and tell me he isn't ready for dinner yet.
4. Cal can say, "Yes, Mom, but I have only one page left, can I please finish the book first?"

What I teach our children is that only options 1 and 4 will bode well for them, and 2 and 3 will lead to disappointment and consequences, every time. "Every time" is the consistency they will learn to not only expect but also respect. Consistency is the key response we need to have to whatever behavior or attitude with which we are challenged.

Interestingly enough, research reveals that "the type of parents who are actually most consistent in enforcing rules are the same parents who are most warm and have the most conversations with their kids."[25] Consistency is associated with warmth and openness in a parent-child relationship. Consistency reflects the heart of Jesus, who "is the same yesterday and today and forever" (Heb. 13:8), and consistency offers our children the ability to learn how to live freely under our, and God's, authority. Consistency in discipline is not oppressive or permissive but rather empowering.

Fairness

Fairness is another important piece to correction and discipline. Fairness essentially means having realistic expectations, because if we are consistent but we are consistent with unrealistic expectations, we can crush our kids' spirits.

Colossians 3:21 is the second of the only two verses in the New Testament with a direct command for parents in childrearing. This verse often gets overlooked but carries such importance, so I want to spend a few moments exploring it with you. "Parents, don't come down too hard on your children or you'll crush their spirits" (Col. 3:21 MSG).

I vividly remember a moment of discipline with Cal when I knew I came down too hard. The look on his beautiful eight-year-old face told me everything I needed to know. I had crushed his spirit, and the conviction of my wrong hit me to the core. Yes, Cal disobeyed me. Yes, Cal disrespected me. And yes, there should have been a conversation about what was going on in his heart and he should have been given consequences. But that wasn't the point in that precise moment. The point was, his disobedience didn't warrant my temper tantrum. And my tantrum definitely wasn't going to lead Cal to a repentant heart. I'd fallen back into unrealistic expectations of perfect obedience from my son, and I had to seek his forgiveness.

Oftentimes, our lack of fairness with our children is rooted in unrealistic expectations. For example, Brennan thinks he's an eight-year-old stuck in a five-year-old's body, and because of this, it's easy for me to forget that he is actually only five. Typically my husband will graciously say, "Wifey, you may be expecting too much of him in this situation. You have to be fair."

But let us not confuse the mistake of having unrealistic expectations with the habit of making excuses for our children. Unrealistic expectations or unachievable standards set our children up for failure. It can crush their spirits. Making excuses for our children, however, is essentially a way of training them how to avoid accountability.

An unrealistic expectation is Mike and I taking our three

children to a restaurant at 8:30 at night and assuming they will behave. Instead, they will be exhausted and starving (because they typically eat at 5:30 and go to bed at 7:30), and they will no longer be capable of making good choices. We will have set the bar too high and doomed them to failure.

But we do not need to make excuses for our children when the expectation is age appropriate and they are fully capable of living up to the standard we have set. The list of excuses includes, "Oh, she is so tired; oh, he is so hungry; oh, he is so shy; oh, he does not like strangers; oh, he is just trying to be funny." And yes, sometimes these are very valid and logical reasons for why our children may be acting like wild monkeys or nervous Nellies. However, more often than not, we make excuses for them because their behavior may cause us embarrassment or shame.

So rather than make excuses for our children, we have to be willing to do the hard work. We must be consistent but fair. We must be firm but gentle. We must be no-nonsense but nurturing. We must continue to discipline them in a way that reflects the heart of Jesus.

Think about this for a moment: What if we looked at moments of disobedience as precious opportunities to reach our kids' hearts instead of seeing their sin or disobedience as personal attacks on us? And what if we used these moments of disobedience as opportunities to train our children not only in righteousness but also in grace? It's about coming alongside our kids and trying to understand the root of their sin,

> We must be consistent but fair. We must be firm but gentle. We must be no-nonsense but nurturing. We must continue to discipline them in a way that reflects the heart of Jesus.

rather than coming at our kids with the stinging accusation of "How could you?" or "Who does something like that?" It's about shifting our focus from forcing change in our kids' outward behavior to reaching their hearts with his grace. It's about pointing our kids back to Jesus as their strength, their righteousness, and their only hope.

Focusing on God's grace caused a radical transformation in my own heart, one that led me to create the "What, Why, How, and Now Discipline Process."

The What, Why, How, and Now of Discipline

When I discipline, I often go through these four steps:

1. *What* are you being disciplined for?
2. *Why* did you disobey?
3. *How* could you have responded?
4. *Now* the consequence.

Let's say I take Owen (who is now four) on a special trip to the park. When it's getting close to the time to leave, I give him a ten-minute warning, and then I give him a five-minute warning. Five minutes later I let Owen know that it's time to go, at which point he has a full-blown temper tantrum and ultimately declares, "I am not leaving!" This is a time when I would walk Owen through the discipline process.

Step 1: What

I ask Owen, "What are you being disciplined for?"

Oftentimes, I find that my children are getting in trouble over and over again for the same thing because they do not fully comprehend what they are doing wrong. What they think they are being corrected for and what I am intending to correct are on two different planets. I have indeed been amazed at some of the answers I have received when I have asked the children, "What did you do or say that required correction?"

Our children need to take ownership of the behavior that requires correction in order for them to learn the lesson we are attempting to teach them, but they can't own a behavior they do not know they are exhibiting. Therefore, if I ask Owen, "What did you do that requires discipline?" and he replies, "I did not want to leave the park," I can ask him leading questions to help him identify the real issue, because it has nothing to do with not wanting to leave the park and everything to do with how he treated me with disrespect and disobedience. This part of the conversation helps to identify the misbehavior and contrast it with the obedience we desire.

Here are a few of the questions I might ask:

- "Owen, are you speaking to Mommy with respect, or are you being rude with your words?"
- "Owen, are you obeying what Mommy asked you to do, or are you arguing with Mommy?"
- "Owen, are you showing thankfulness for the fun time we had at the park, or are you just focused on having more?"

Step 2: Why

Next I ask Owen, "Why did you disobey?"

Oh, how I love this part of the conversation. Yes, really, I love this part, because it focuses on the heart, the belief behind the behavior. The answer to this question points us back to Jesus and his extravagant grace. The answer to the question, "Why did you disobey?" is pretty much the same every time I ask it, no matter what the offense. "Because I'm not perfect." And this is the same answer I would give you if you asked me why *I* disobeyed my Savior today. "Because I'm not perfect."

Owen disobeyed, just as I disobey, because as sinners, our hearts are prone to wander and rebel. As sinners, our hearts are inclined to selfish desires and wants. And as sinners, what we should do and what we want to do are always at war within us. "Be perfect, therefore, as your heavenly Father is perfect" (Matt. 5:48) is possible only because Jesus stands in the gap between my sin and God's righteousness and proclaims, "I have her covered!"

> "Be perfect, therefore, as your heavenly Father is perfect" (Matt. 5:48) is possible only because Jesus stands in the gap between my sin and God's righteousness and proclaims, "I have her covered!"

This is where I can remind Owen that though he is indeed wonderfully and oh so perfectly made in God's very own image, I don't expect him to behave perfectly or to obey me perfectly every time. It's simply not possible. (This is not excusing or endorsing the sin but acknowledging the reality of our fallen human nature.) And I can remind him that he is still my beloved son and I am no less pleased with him, but as his mom I must still discipline the disobedience and point him to the only one who can give him the desire and the power to obey God's Word and honor me as his mother.

Therefore, asking Owen, "Why did you disobey?" reminds both of us that we are sinners in need of a Savior, and a Savior we do indeed have in Jesus Christ, who offers us a divine exchange of our sins for his perfect righteousness, and names us beloved children of God.

Step 3: How

Next I ask Owen how he could have responded differently in that situation.

Another benefit of discipline is that it offers us an opportunity to retrain our children in the way they should go. A simple "What could you have done differently in that situation?" or "How could you have handled that better?" goes a very long way.

Oftentimes we will role-play the *how*. For instance, I can say to Owen, "Now please show me how you could have spoken differently to me." We work together to come up with the words he could have used or the attitude or tone that would have been acceptable. Role-playing the very thing he should have done increases the chances that he will get it right the next time.

This part of the conversation is an awesome opportunity to share Bible verses with your children to instruct them in the truth and grace of Scripture. This can also be a good opportunity to talk with our kids about whether they asked Jesus to help them in this circumstance. And if the answer is no, we can gently encourage our kids to rely on the Holy Spirit to change their hearts and give them a willing spirit.

Step 4: Now

Now the consequence.

Let me begin by saying that there may not always be some big grand consequence. Sometimes the consequence is the conversation itself. Sometimes, in walking our kids through this process, the Holy Spirit convicts their hearts, they show genuine repentance, and the work is done. This is typically when I offer our kids what I call a "mercy moment." I remind them that just as the Lord's "mercies begin afresh each morning" (Lam 3:22–23 NLT), Mommy is going to do the same. And rarely do I regret showing mercy.

> We can offer our kids "mercy moments" to remind them of the mercies of Christ, which are new every morning.

However, when you do need to have more than just a conversation as a consequence, I would encourage you to choose logical consequences whenever possible. Logical consequences are consequences that correlate with the behavior that requires discipline. They are not essential, but there are plenty of good reasons to prove they can be helpful, primarily because they remind children that poor choices equal poor outcomes.

In the park scenario, I explained to Owen that we would have to play in our own yard the following day, and if he obeyed me and treated me with respect when I told him to come inside, we would give the park another shot. But until I could trust that he would show thankfulness and respect next time we visited the park, I removed the privilege of going there. The loss of a privilege is only one of the many forms of discipline I could have chosen, but it was the most logical one for the situation.

Types of Discipline

It goes without saying that children respond differently to the various types of discipline. By trial and error, I have learned what type of discipline is most effective with each child, and this knowledge guides my choices in how I discipline them.

We all know the various types of discipline we can choose from for our young children, the most common being time-outs, loss of privileges, and spankings. Plenty of books already have been written that can help you decide which form of discipline is best for your child and what the Bible says about each of them. As you well know, opinions vary greatly on this topic.

My intention is not to dig into the types of discipline from which we can choose but, more important, to get right to the heart of our motivation for discipline, as this has been the most helpful for me in determining how to discipline my children in light of God's holy discipline in my own life.

Motivation and Implementation

However we choose to discipline our children, our motivation and implementation are key. To assess our motivation, an important question to ask ourselves is, "What is my goal in discipline?"

See, before I understood God's grace in my life, my goal in discipline was to change my kids, to force them to obey, to instill fear of consequences, and quite honestly, to make my life easier. My motives weren't pure, and it boiled over into my actions.

To reflect the heart of Jesus, our motive in discipline must be to help our children identify their behavior or sin, and if they are old enough, instill godly sorrow. To assess your motive, ask yourself, "Am I pointing my kids back to Jesus and what he has already done for them through his life, death, and resurrection?" Drop the guilt and shame trips. Shame ultimately leads our children into desperation and sin, but godly sorrow produces a harvest of righteousness. "For the kind of sorrow God wants us to experience leads us away from sin and results in salvation. There's no regret for that kind of sorrow" (2 Cor. 7:10 NLT).

> Drop the guilt and shame trips. Shame ultimately leads our children deeper into desperation and sin, but godly sorrow produces a harvest of righteousness.

Remember, while their sin may require consequences, there is no condemnation in Christ. We must give them both truth and grace, then allow their hearts to be transformed through the power of the Holy Spirit.

Our implementation must be firm but gentle. We will never (ever!) reach our children's hearts when we discipline in anger or as a means of venting our frustration toward their behavior. This approach will only incite, humiliate, or shame our children, which is certainly not the template we want to create for our children to understand God's holy discipline in our lives. Remember, the kindness of the Lord is meant to lead us to repentance (Rom. 2:4). Implement discipline from that lens.

And finally, in times of discipline, when possible, we need to offer our children the dignity of being disciplined privately. A public display of discipline can feel very shaming to a child. And if we can't have privacy, whispering is a good second option.

Our children are much more likely to receive whatever we are desiring to teach them in our discipline when we reflect the heart of Jesus in our approach and lead with love unconditional.

chapter 21

repentance and forgiveness

Bear with each other and forgive one another
if any of you has a grievance against someone.
Forgive as the Lord forgave you.
—Colossians 3:13

When my father, who is a pastor, married Mike and me ten years ago, he did a short homily about the nine hardest words in the English language. The nine words are *I am sorry, I am wrong, please forgive me*. In our early days of marriage, I quickly learned how to turn those nine words into these eleven words: *I am sorry that you were wrong, I will forgive you*. No, *sorry* was not my forte. But the truth is if I want to model a life in Christ for my kids, I must be willing to model the nine hardest words.

Ending the conversation after discipline and correction is not the standard God has set for us. The discipline process should always lead to repentance, forgiveness, and a restoration of relationship. We forgive because he freely forgives us; in fact, he lavishly forgives. Helping our children understand the forgiveness and compassion of Christ begins in our willingness to model our own need for forgiveness, our own need for a Savior. We have to be willing to model a humble and contrite heart, the kind of heart that David reveals in Psalm 51:1–4: "Have mercy on me, O God, according to your unfailing love; according to your great compassion blot out my transgressions. Wash away all my iniquity and cleanse me from my sin. For I know my transgressions, and my sin is always before me. Against you, you only, have I sinned and done what is evil in your sight."

Of course our children can't possibly appreciate this prayer just yet, but oh, they will one day. As they come to understand the power of sin, and the grip it can have on us, they will come to love this prayer. In the meantime, we can teach our children about God's

> We can teach our children about God's unfailing love and the delight he finds in a contrite and repentant heart.

unfailing love and the delight he finds in a contrite and repentant heart. Our children can learn that even someone like David, whom God called "a man after my own heart," desperately needed God's forgiveness. And God lavishly poured it out on him.

Not only do our children need to see our willingness to seek forgiveness from Jesus but they also need to see us seeking forgiveness from one another and from them.

Be Willing to Model a Repentant Heart

Sitting at my good friend's kitchen table, I felt cranky and overwhelmed by some of the circumstances our family was facing. (That's what happens when I'm not fully trusting God!) As I was recounting the details of the day to my friends at the table, I let a word roll off my tongue that I don't allow my kids to use. And before I could get another word out, I heard a sweet little voice from behind me say, "Mom, I heard that."

I turned to see Cal sitting at the table in the next room playing Legos and listening intently to my every word.

"You heard what, Cal?"

"I heard what you said, Mom."

"What did I say, Cal?"

"You know, Mom."

"No, I don't, Cal."

"Yes, you do, Mom." And he turned back to his Legos.

I sat there thinking, "Wow. I just turned into an eight-year-old bantering with another eight-year-old: 'Yes, you did.' 'No, I didn't.' 'Yes, you did.' 'No, I didn't.'"

I mouthed, "Busted!" to my friends sitting at the table with me. And though I tried to continue the conversation, the conviction came quickly. I knew what I had to do, so I asked Cal to join me in the next room alone.

I sat face-to-face with my precious son and confessed, "Cal, Mommy needs to apologize and ask for your forgiveness. I used a word I have taught you not to say, and then I was not honest about it when you told me you heard me say it."

> Modeling a life in Christ for our kids is not about always getting it right. If it were, I would have given up a long time ago.

And then I offered Cal the nine hardest words: "I am sorry. I was wrong. Please forgive me."

What I am learning is that modeling a life in Christ for our kids is not about always getting it right. If it were, I would have given up a long time ago. No, modeling a life in Christ is mostly about modeling how much we need Jesus.

We need Jesus to help us live like he did. We need the power of the Holy Spirit to convict, melt, and transform our hearts over and over again to mold us into his image. And we need his sweet, sweet sacrifice on the cross for when we fail. We need his strength for when we are weak. We need his hope for when we feel hopeless. We need his love for when we feel loveless.

We need his grace.

So after I offered the nine hardest words to Cal, I reminded Cal that Mommy is a sinner who needs a Savior by whispering in his ear, "Thank God for Jesus."

As much as I desire to model the kind of life Jesus calls us to live as his disciples, I have to daily remind myself that Jesus didn't say, "They will know you are my disciples by your perfection." No, he said, "They will know you are my disciples by your love" (see John 13:35).

Jesus is my kids' perfect example. And more than that, he is my kids' faithful and loving Savior. I can do my best to reflect his life and his heart to my kids, but I will fail. I am human, I am fallen, and I need my Savior, just as they are human and fallen and need their Savior. And because of what he did for us on the cross—a divine exchange of our sin for his perfect righteousness—I am set free to confess my sin to my son and to my Savior and know that I am fully covered and fully forgiven in Christ.

When I was done with my apology, Cal hugged me tight and whispered, "It's okay, Mommy. I forgive you."

With a full heart, I replied, "Thank you, baby. I love you so much."

The Difference between Repentance and an Apology

Understanding the difference between repentance and an apology is crucial in training our children in this area. In the simplest of terms, *repentance* can be described as a deep sorrow for wrongdoing that leads to a change of heart. In fact the word *repent* comes from the Greek word *metanoia*, which means "to have a change of heart." Repentance brings a sorrow that turns us away from our sin and toward God, as illustrated in Psalm 51. It is a broken spirit, a heart that is deeply grieved by sin, and a desperate longing to be restored.

An apology, on the other hand, is sometimes a result of a repentant heart, and sometimes it is an act of the will. For example, if our young children cannot, or do not, feel godly sorrow for their wrongdoing, we can still train them to apologize long before they understand why an apology is necessary, and how to seek forgiveness long before they understand its benefits.

But what about older children who are able to link belief to behavior and do understand how their actions require an apology but still refuse? We can start with the hard "why" question—"Why don't you want to apologize?"—to help them identify the sin in their heart that is causing their behavior. And if there is still work to do, perhaps we might say something like, "That was not a respectful way to speak to me, and I love you too much to allow you to treat me that way. Would you like to apologize to me now or would you like to go to your room to think through your actions and come back when you're ready to apologize?" Or, "You are not allowed to tear down your brother with your words. I know you know the right thing to do, but since you are not ready to apologize, please go to your room and pray that the Holy Spirit will show you your need for forgiveness, and come back when you're ready."

> In training our children to apologize, we open the door for them to experience the great freedom in confessing wrongdoing and receiving forgiveness for it.

You see, while we cannot force our children into repentance (which can only be the result of the Holy Spirit at work in their hearts), we can require that they apologize for their offense. When we enforce this, we need to remember that our child's "I am sorry" need not be said from a deep sense of one's shortcomings. Often, as I said, the "I am sorry" is offered as an act of the will. Our children should not have the luxury of withholding an apology until they "feel like it." They may need a little time to think about it, and a little time is given to them, but ultimately it is the conformity of the will, not their personal emotional sensitivity to the wrong they are doing, that offers the "I am sorry." In training our children to apologize, we open the door for them to experience the great freedom in confessing wrongdoing and receiving forgiveness for it.

Be Specific with the Apology

When we, or our children, apologize, it is never enough to flippantly say sorry and walk away. For instance, in the above scenario, my apology to Cal began with, "I used a word I have taught you not to say, and then I was not honest about it when you told me you heard me say it." I took accountability for my wrongdoing and was specific about that for which I sought forgiveness. Taking the time to identify our specific sin or wrongdoing is an essential part of moving our hearts from an act of the will to repentance that culminates in forgiveness and restoration of the relationship. Whether our children admit it or not, they long for restored relationship. We all long for restored relationship, for things to be made right. And they rely on us to lead them in that restored relationship with one another.

Offer Forgiveness

Teaching our children to respond with forgiveness begins with teaching them what forgiveness means and how forgiveness is crucial to restored relationship. Forgiveness is not justification or endorsement of sin. This is important for our children to understand. The act of forgiveness is a response of love that flows from the forgiveness God so lavishly extends to us in Jesus Christ. So instead of allowing our children to huff about self-righteously or hold a grudge, we need to teach them to forgive one another in light of the forgiveness Jesus extends to us.

> The act of forgiveness is a response of love that flows from the forgiveness God so lavishly extends to us in Jesus Christ.

When we reflect on our own brokenness, we are more compassionate toward the brokenness of others and how their brokenness impacts us. When we keep our eyes on the cross, our own need for forgiveness is revealed and satisfied. And as parents, we have a precious opportunity to model this kind of forgiveness for our kids, setting an example of how they can forgive one another and experience restored relationship.

For example, during a recent morning walk to school, Brennan's frustration grew with each step we took. He didn't have a play date scheduled after school, he didn't like what I'd packed him for snack, and he definitely didn't want to go to T-ball practice after school. It was one of those mornings when he felt like the world was his enemy. When we arrived at school, I gave Cal a hug and kiss as I always do and sent him on his way. But on this particular day Brennan saw this moment as a fine opportunity to kick me (albeit gently) in the ankle. I turned to Brennan, fully prepared to address his actions with corrective words, but before I could say a word, grace washed over me.

By the grace of God, words came out of my mouth that were not my own. I simply said, "Honey, you have to go to school now. There isn't time for us to talk about what's happening in your heart that's causing you to complain and show such disrespect to Mommy, but before I send you into the building, I want you to know this very important thing: I have a feeling that when you get into your classroom, and you sit down at your desk, you are going to be sad and feel bad about the way you just treated Mommy. I know this because I know your beautiful heart and I know you love me and don't want to treat me this way. So when that sadness hits you, I want you to remember that I love you and I have already forgiven you." And I prayed in his ear, "Jesus, please bless my beautiful son today, whom I know you love even more than I do."

And immediately, and I mean immediately, my son melted into my arms. Grace washed over him too. His hard heart was broken with grace, and no more words were spoken. I held him for a moment while tears streamed down his cheeks, and then he walked into the building, but before he turned the corner, he turned to show me his face. We smiled at one another. My heart was full. We were both thankful for forgiveness and restored relationship. And showing one another this kind of grace is possible only when we reflect on our own brokenness and the mercy we've been shown through Christ.

Pray

In times of repentance and forgiveness, praying together is a gift. Because of what Jesus Christ has done for us, we are free to confess our sin to each other, and to confess our sin to God.

If we lack repentant hearts—if our "sorry" comes as an act of the will more than from a sorrow for our sin—we begin by praying for a contrite and repentant heart, a heart that is grieved by the same things that grieve the heart of Jesus.

If we have grudge-holding hearts—if our "I forgive you" comes as an act of the will more than a desire to extend mercy—we begin by praying for a softened heart filled with love, a heart that extends the same forgiveness that Jesus gave to us.

In prayer we receive and celebrate the forgiveness Jesus has already extended to us through his death on the cross and his resurrection.

We thank him for being the offering for our sin. We thank him for his grace and mercy that flow so freely when we repent.

Bury the Sin

Just as Jesus buries our sins in the depths of the sea and remembers them no more, so we can do the same with one another. As we read in Micah 7:19 (NLT), "Once again you will have compassion on us. You will trample our sins under your feet and throw them into the depths of the ocean!"

Our children know that, in the priceless words of Corrie ten Boom, there is "No fishing allowed." This means that we not only forgive the sin but we also don't go fishing for past sins when we want to use them against someone in the future. We surrender it. The offender and the offended are set free from the bitterness that prospers where grace is lacking (Heb. 12:15). What better way is there to reflect God's heart of unconditional love toward our children than to wipe the slate clean? From his extravagant grace flows extravagant forgiveness.

God's Final Word

God's extravagant grace forever eliminates the burden of perfection and performance, and it compels us and our children to live out of the freedom and fullness of his wholehearted and unconditional love in Christ Jesus.

Grace is God's final word: You are fully accepted and fully forgiven. Fully known and fully loved. Not because of what you do for Jesus but because of what Jesus has already done for you. Let your heart be wrecked afresh as you revel in this radical grace and stand amazed at how it captivates your child's heart.

epilogue:
how to get started
parenting a
wholehearted child

Children are a gift from the LORD;
they are a reward from him.
—Psalm 127:3 NLT

Together we can raise up a generation of *not perfect* but whole-hearted children, children who live from the freedom found in being wholeheartedly and unconditionally loved (and liked!) by God in Jesus Christ.

We can say "enough!" to the joy-robbing pressure to be perfect parents raising perfect kids. Instead, we can free-fall into the arms of grace. We can smile in the assurance that as much as we love our children, Jesus loves them infinitely more. And we can bear witness to what happens when the fullness of his love inspires and compels sacrificial and self-giving love in our children for Christ and for others. By the power of his Spirit, he can transform their hearts with his grace in ways we might not be bold enough to dream.

If you want to join me in this transformative journey, I offer a few ideas below that I hope will help you get started. This is not a checklist or a formula but merely a reflection of our family's ongoing journey that I pray might also help your family grow in grace.

- *Identify your starting place.* Begin by reflecting on these questions: In what have we been discipling our children? What is our purpose in parenting? What would it look like if we made grace (the one-way love of Jesus) our starting place?

- *Help your children develop a trusting relationship with Jesus.* Reflect on the ways in which you can affirm your children's identity in Christ, lead them in putting their trust in him, and empower them in growing in a vibrant friendship with him. Sow seeds of faith (prayer, Bible reading, Scripture memorization, worship and community, and service) into your family life to nurture your and your children's relationship with Jesus.

- *Choose a family Bible verse and virtues.* Start this process with prayer. Ask God to lead you in seeking his heart for your family. Reflect on who your children are and who you want to help them become, the kind of heart you hope they will have and the kind of faith and character you hope to help them develop. Remember, this process has nothing to do with creating perfectly behaved children and everything to do with giving them a foundation of grace from which they can grow in a vibrant friendship with Jesus and grow in his likeness.

- *Involve your children in the discussion.* Talk to your children about the reasons you are identifying virtues for growing in Christlike character and give them an opportunity to contribute to the conversation. Ask them what they think is important in your home and what they think the Bible teaches us about the promises and commandments of Christ. Having this type of conversation is a window into the messages you have been sending your children. You may be pleasantly amazed by what you have been teaching them, or perhaps it will frighten you, as it did me. It definitely helped us identify why we were struggling in some areas and thriving in others. Most important, make sure they know that their input into this process is precious and valuable. Having a sense of ownership can only be a good thing!

- *Lead with love unconditional.* Remember the awesome privilege you have in reflecting the heart of Jesus to your children. The way in which you lead your children through authority and obedience, instruction and training, discipline and correction, and repentance and forgiveness will bear witness to the unconditional nature of Christ's love. Give your children the wholehearted and unconditional love of Jesus, which motivates and compels love for him and for others.

- *Surrender!* Prying my fingers, one by one, off the rock of self-reliance that I'm so prone to cling to, and surrendering my children back into the hands of Christ, is accomplished only through prayer. Ironic, isn't it, that it's much easier to pretend like we can change our children than it is to trust Jesus to do what only he can do in our children's hearts through grace.

The most important thing we can do for our kids is captivate them with what Jesus has already done for them. That is the essence of raising a wholehearted child. Give your kids grace, and don't just settle for the shallow waters of grace. Dive into the deep end and see if it doesn't change you, and your kids, from the inside out.

Remember, the Lord's mercies are new *every* morning. And he is ever faithful to his promises.

> The most important thing we can do for our kids is captivate them with what Jesus has already done for them.

Hear his tender voice reminding you, "Your children are a gift from me; they are a reward from the Father! Enjoy them! Give them grace, and take refuge in the shadow of my wings. Trust in my unfathomable love for them—and for you."

"Because of the LORD's great love we are not consumed, for his compassions never fail. They are new every morning; great is your faithfulness" (Lam. 3:22–23).

notes

1. Paul Zahl, *Grace in Practice* (Grand Rapids, Mich.: Eerdmans, 2007), 38.
2. Elyse Fitzpatrick, *Counsel from the Cross* (Wheaton, Ill.: Crossway, 2009), 25.
3. Kara Powell and Chap Clark, *Sticky Faith* (Grand Rapids, Mich.: Zondervan, 2011), 15.
4. John Eldredge, *Beautiful Outlaw* (Nashville: FaithWords, 2012), 12.
5. Beth Moore, *Believing God Workbook* (Nashville: Broadman, 2004), 85.
6. Brennan Manning, *The Relentless Tenderness of Jesus* (Grand Rapids, Mich.: Revell, 1986, 2004), 25.
7. Brennan Manning, *The Furious Longing of God* (Colorado Springs: Cook, 2009), 75.
8. Max Lucado, *Grace* (Nashville: Thomas Nelson, 2012), 124.
9. Jodie Berndt, *Praying the Scriptures for Your Children* (Grand Rapids, Mich.: Zondervan, 2001), 23.
10. Sally Lloyd-Jones, *The Jesus Storybook Bible* (Grand Rapids, Mich.: Zondervan, 2007), 226.
11. Ibid., 14–17.

12. Charles R. Swindoll, *Growing Strong in the Seasons of Life* (Grand Rapids, Mich.: Zondervan, 1983), 61.

13. Powell and Clark, *Sticky Faith*, 97.

14. Manning, *Furious Longing of God*, 120.

15. You can find details of Courtney Defeo's extraordinary adventure on her website, *http://courtneydefeo.com/light-em-up-2012*.

16. Po Bronson and Ashley Merryman, *Nurture Shock* (New York: Hachette, 2011), 121.

17. Todd Cartmell, *Keep the Siblings, Lose the Rivalry* (Grand Rapids, Mich.: Zondervan, 2003), 59–71.

18. Ann Voskamp, *One Thousand Gifts* (Grand Rapids, Mich.: Zondervan, 2011), 36.

19. Bronson and Merryman, *Nurture Shock*, 84–85.

20. Tedd Tripp, *Shepherding a Child's Heart* (Wapwallopen, Pa.: Shepherd Press, 1995), xviii.

21. Ibid., 138.

22. Elyse Fitzpatrick and Jessica Thompson, *Give Them Grace* (Wheaton, Ill.: Crossway, 2011), 94.

23. Ibid., 99.

24. James Dobson, *Dare to Discipline* (Wheaton, Ill.: Tyndale, 1996), 36.

25. Bronson and Merryman, *Nurture Shock*, 140.